Semiotics and Title Sequences

Title sequences are the most obvious place where photography and typography combine on-screen, yet they are also a commonly neglected part of film studies. *Semiotics and Title Sequences* presents the first theoretical model and historical consideration of how text and image combine to create meaning in title sequences for film and television, before extending its analysis to include subtitles, intertitles, and the narrative role for typography. Detailed close readings of classic films starting with *The Cabinet of Dr. Caligari*, and including *To Kill a Mockingbird*, *Dr. Strangelove*, and *The Good, the Bad, and the Ugly*, along with designs from television programs such as *Magnum P.I.*, *Castle*, and *Vikings* present a critical assessment of title sequences as both an independent art form and an introduction to the film that follows.

Michael Betancourt is an artist/theorist concerned with digital technology and capitalist ideology. His writing has been translated into Chinese, French, Greek, Italian, Japanese, Persian, Portuguese, and Spanish, and been published in magazines such as *The Atlantic*, *Make Magazine*, *Millennium Film Journal*, *Leonardo*, *Semiotica*, and *CTheory*. He wrote *The ___________ Manifesto*, and other books such as *The Critique of Digital Capitalism*, *The History of Motion Graphics*, *Glitch Art in Theory and Practice*, and *Beyond Spatial Montage: Windowing*. These publications complement his movies, which have screened internationally at the Black Maria Film Festival, Art Basel Miami Beach, Contemporary Art Ruhr, Athens Video Art Festival, Festival des Cinemas Differents de Paris, Anthology Film Archives, Millennium Film Workshop, the San Francisco Cinematheque's Crossroads, and Experiments in Cinema, among many others.

Routledge Studies in Media Theory & Practice

1 **Semiotics and Title Sequences**
Text–Image Composites in Motion Graphics
Authored by Michael Betancourt

Semiotics and Title Sequences

Text–Image Composites in Motion Graphics

Michael Betancourt

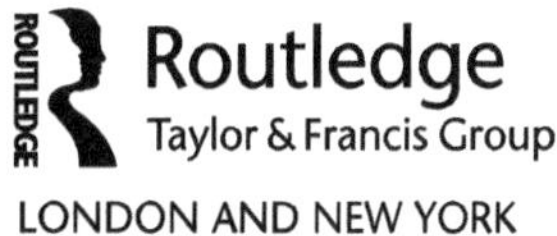

LONDON AND NEW YORK

First published 2017
by Routledge

2 Park Square, Milton Park, Abingdon, Oxfordshire OX14 4RN
52 Vanderbilt Avenue, New York, NY 10017

Routledge is an imprint of the Taylor & Francis Group, an informa business

First issued in paperback 2019

Some sections of this book were adapted from previously published essays produced in earlier stages of this analysis:

"The Calligram and the Title Card," in *Semiotica: Journal of the International Association for Semiotic Studies*, no. 204, pp. 239–252, 2015.

"Frame Analysis: The Title Sequence for Doris Wishman's *Bad Girls Go to Hell* (1965)," in *Bright Lights Film Journal*, June 3, 2014.

"Pablo Ferro's Title Montage for *Bullitt* (1968): The Criminality Beneath the Surface of Civil Society," in *Bright Lights Film Journal*, April 29, 2014.

"The Horror of Origins: Ron Honthaner's *The House on Skull Mountain*," in *Bright Lights Film Journal*, issue 82, November, 2013.

"Lardani's Signature: Technical Mastery and Apparent Glitch in Eugenio Lardani's titles for Sergio Leone's *The Good, The Bad, and The Ugly*," in *Bright Lights Film Journal*, issue 81, August, 2013.

Library of Congress Cataloging-in-Publication Data
A catalog record for this book has been requested

ISBN: 978-1-138-63420-6 (hbk)
ISBN: 978-0-367-88755-1 (pbk)

Typeset in Times New Roman
by Apex CoVantage, LLC

For Leah

Contents

Figures

Acknowledgments

This book would not have been possible without the discussions with my graduate students, especially Dominica Jordan, Preston Gibson, Eric Dies, Patrick Shanholtzer, and Noël Anderson; and my colleagues Min Ho Shin and Duff Yong. Special thanks go to my brother, John Betancourt, for his assistance with locating the title sequences that inform this study.

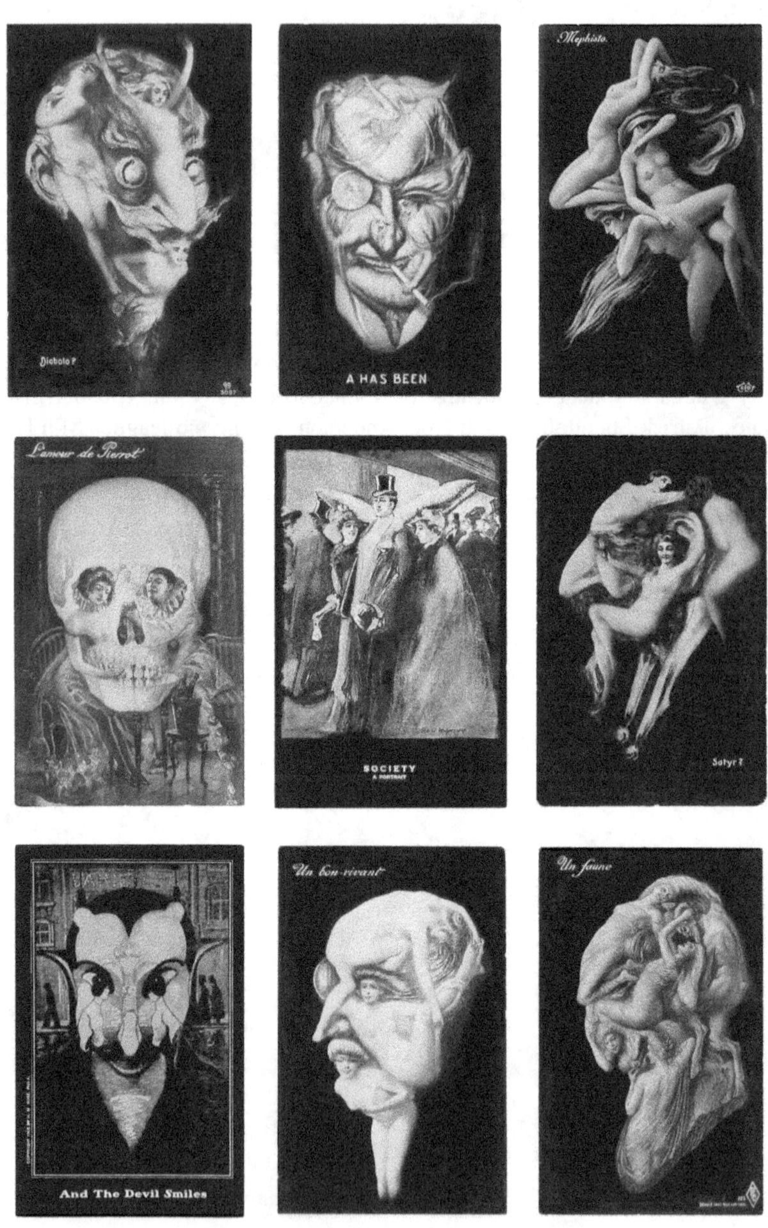

Frontis A selection of metamorphic illusion postcards, c. 1890–1910

1

This book emerged from fragmentary work done over several years concerned with the relationship between meaning and form in title sequence designs (mostly) produced for feature films and television programs in the United States. Some of the individual close readings that appear in this book have been published as self-contained considerations of specific title designs, while for many others, this is their first time appearing publicly. The foundations of this analysis lie with the history of title designs in film, television, and video games developed in my monograph *The History of Motion Graphics: From Avant-Garde to Industry in the United States*. Proposing a general semiotic theory for title sequences and other arrangements of text and image on-screen originates with this same analysis and research. However, the application of semiotics to composites of text–imagery is not limited to title designs, but can be applied to all motion graphics such as subtitles, intertitles, as well as any other text on-screen, and potentially even to similar visual structures in graphic design. The three general modes presented in this study are easily recognizable in title sequences. The critical extension of these same structures to describing text–image composites, such as subtitles, follows from these more prominent applications: title sequences offer the greatest variety of uses and designs employing the three fundamental modes. The proposed semiotic theory of text–image composition is generalized from studies of particular designs chosen for their typicality.

All title sequences are marginal productions—whether produced for film, television, video games, or any other media—these *paratexts*[1] come at either the start or end of the narrative, attached to yet also independent of the main production. Yet they occupy a difficult middle ground between being autonomous and integrated; they are not independent productions, but are often made independently of the drama or narrative.[2] The careful, close consideration of these designs illuminates the complexity of this dynamic, allowing for a theoretical understanding of the semiotic relationships possible with composites of text and image. While the consideration of title sequences is the main focus of this analysis, it also includes the logical extension of this theory into title montages, subtitles, and related forms combining text and image.

Although sound and music also play a major (and prominent) role in the design, production, and organization of title sequences (and all motion graphics generally), this study is not primarily focused on the semiotics of audio-visual relationships. Their discussion are *en passant* observations included in the interests of thoroughness: the soundtrack is part of the meaning emergent from title sequences, yet a full and complete consideration of sound is beyond the scope of the present analysis—the essential element of title design is text, *not* sound. The theory proposed in this book is concerned with the on-screen relationship and organization of text in relation to a background image. Some title designs are elaborately synchronized to their score, while others are silent. Both the soundtrack and background images can be removed from the title sequence without fundamentally destroying what defines the title sequence as a *title*—but to remove the *type* transforms the title design into something else—an animated film, or perhaps a standard montage. Even in the title design used for the television program *Castle* that has no credits and only concludes with an animated logo, the presence of the logo (the text) is the necessary and sufficient condition required for the sequence being identified *as* a title sequence. *Text* is the crucial element that cannot be removed, but the semiotics surrounding it are neither critically well described nor comprehensively theorized.

Yet, the title sequence *is* a hybrid construction and this intermedial nature *is* a mixture of music, written language (texts), and visual materials of various types, both live action and animated, composited to create the singular units called "title cards." Their organization into the totality of a title sequence is more than just an arbitrary arrangement of pieces or a montage of shots. The order of the cards, their duration, the size of names, and their separation/combination into each card is governed by a maze of traditions, contractual obligations, and individual temperaments. While these factors constrain the design, limiting and focusing it in advance of its production in ways separate from the actual title sequence, the finished result is *other* than simply a sum of these varied and cacophonous demands. A close reading thus comes as the preferred solution to address these complexities, allowing for a consideration of each design as an artifact requiring its own nuanced analysis in context with other similar designs, while allowing for the generalizations that link theory to practice.

Commonalities of approach and engagement emerge from these repeated considerations: the present theorization follows from individual analyses augmented by contextual research across the history and range of title designs made in the United States, rather than being limited to just the already-known work of "star" designers, or those famous designs created by uncredited designers working on well-known and regarded films. This analysis focuses on a variety of typical designs from film and television chosen precisely because they can serve as general examples of type. This selection process required looking at a broad range of designs with as much attention paid to monotonous, minor works as to major, well-known designs. By including these other sequences that are commonly ignored as uninteresting and insignificant because they do not offer much for a close reading, the proposed semiotic theory for composites of text and image is meant to be general in scope: the meaning-producing modes described by this analysis of title sequence designs can be extended to include any composites of text and image, not just those employed by/in motion pictures.

Theory and Design

When theories of design address typography, the tendency is to consider legibility and then move on to other, more general and abstract approaches to composition and organization. This concern with formal principles of arrangement is accompanied by a metaphysical conception of design devoid of cultural signification. It is an approach to typographics that systematically ignores and rejects the significance of even clearly symbolic imagery. Paul Rand, a prolific theorist of this approach, is typical in his off-hand dismissal of self-evident religious iconography in *Thoughts on Design* (1970):

> It is significant that the crucifix, aside from its religious implications, is a demonstration of perfect form as well—a union of the aggressive vertical (male) and the passive horizontal (female). It is not too farfetched to infer that these formal relations have at least something to do with its enduring quality.[3]

Rand's formalist metaphysics elides the central place this religious symbol has in relation to the various Christian faiths in favor of a sexist overlay of his own symbolic metaphysics onto a cultural artifact. This totalizing conception of formalism necessarily destroys the historical and enduring factors of iconography and tradition, replacing them with his own invention. It is a constructive denial that negates earlier symbolisms and meanings since it enables the development of his theory without concern for the complexities of semiotics and exigencies of established meaning and tradition that constrain interpretation. The approach that Rand adopts is common in theorizations of design: they tend towards this precise formalist vacuum when confronting established meaning and symbolic form. These constraints become especially apparent when design theory encounters typography.

Gygory Kepes's series of monographs on various aspects of design published throughout his career are strikingly devoid of considerations of typography. Neither his anthologies such as *Sign Image Symbol* (1966) nor his own book *Language of Vision* (1959) contain theoretical analyses of typography in design. The closest discussion in his anthologies appears in the article "Case Study: Symbols for Industrial Use" by industrial designer Henry Dreyfuss that presents a discussion of his own work with developing symbols for use on machinery. Dreyfuss does not propose a theory, offering instead only a series of personal guidelines and examples he used in his work.

Even in contemporary studies of graphic design, the focus tends towards a formalist discussion of potential arrangements and structural organization rather than theory. In *Modern Typography* Robin Kinross presents a historical account of how typography developed over the five centuries from Guttenberg's press to the present day. This focus on formal development is common. Even when theories such as deconstruction are considered in Ellen Lupton and Abbott Miller's *Design Writing Research: Writing on Graphic Design*, published in 1996, their study does *not* engage in theory or theorizing design, but describes what theory might provide to a critical understanding *of* design; however, their analysis is confined to the introduction. It is a history tempered by theoretical questions, not a theory engaged with or of design. The rest of the book returns to model examples chosen for their formal development and arrangement of graphics and type. The introductory theoretical foundation defines concepts that provide a critical context for their close analysis of particular designs without proposing general principles. While Lupton and Miller's introduction identifies a material linkage between the organization of typography and its meaning that is independent of the words themselves, their approach remains taxonomic:

> Spacing and punctuation, borders and frames: these are the territory of typography and graphic design, those marginal arts that render texts and images readable. The substance of typography lies not in the alphabet as such—the generic forms of characters and their conventional uses—but rather in the framework and specific graphic forms that materialize the system of writing. Design and typography work at the *edges* of writing, determining the shape and style of letters, the spaces between them, and their placement on the page. Typography, from its position at the margins of communication, has moved writing away from speech.[4]

They recognize the importance of design as a mediation of meaning, but fall back into the traditional formalist approach; the theory their discussion implies never emerges. Lupton and Miller's analysis in *Design Writing*

Research: Writing on Graphic Design is typical of how theory appears in discussion of design: it does not *theorize* as such—instead of theory, these books collect and organize hierarchies of material, formal taxonomies of examples, which are then arranged and considered as a lexicon of model approaches, commonly presented as historical accounts of exceptional designs produced by skilled practitioners. Their audience is specifically practitioners; thus, rather than providing a thorough theory, it suggests a useful and intelligent history of graphic design's encounter with post-modernism. Their considerations of model designs is focused on how they have revealed, revised, or challenged accepted rules—but does not address the underlying theoretical issues: *what are these rules, why do they function as they do?*

As film historian Jan-Christopher Horak noted in his book *Saul Bass: Anatomy of Film Design*, there are no academic theories of film titles, and the formal consideration of *kinetic* typography or its role in design is rare. The relative independence of title sequence designs from the dramatic narratives that follow them has allowed a degree of formal experimentation atypical of these productions generally. Yet, formal theories of film title design are also notably absent from film theory: in place of such considerations are a collection of traditional views about the "ideal" relationship between title sequence and dramatic narrative that have been circulating since at least the 1950s; Georg Stanitzek's analysis in his article "Reading the Title Sequence (Vorspann, Génèrique)" is typical, providing a series of observations that affirm these established traditions. Film studies tends to consider title design as a variety of *paratext*: a reflection on the main production following (or separate from) the title design, as a subservient form best understood through its narrative relationship to the primary production.[5] Approaching title sequences as unique objects,[6] rather than developing any general theories of their design or constitution, follows the traditions of graphic design that focuses on models to emulate. Other books on film titles, such as *Uncredited: Graphic Design and Opening Titles in Movies* by Gemma Solana and Antonio Boneu, are illustrated surveys of interesting designs: what established hagiographies of title designs provide is a specific collection of noteworthy designers—Saul Bass, Maurice Binder, Pablo Ferro, et al. who also typically received prominent, on-screen credit for their work. Critical discussions such as Anna Zagala's brief article "The Edges of Film" in *Sense of Cinema* are cursory, offering only suggestions that a theoretical analysis of title sequences is possible:

> Films variously incorporate titles as discrete and separate sequences preceding the live action, as text superimposed over early, often ambient, establishing shots, or combine these two approaches in hybrid forms.

> The diverse approaches to film title design reflects not only innovation but also a certain dis-ease. In film title sequences the relationship between image and type is always an uneasy one. Foucault in his essay on Magritte's painting "This is not a pipe" characterizes the relationship between text and image in Western painting as necessarily hierarchical in which one is always dominated by the other. Foucault acknowledges that this relationship is rarely stable but that what is vital is that the verbal signs and visual representations are never given at once. It's a dynamic that Deleuze, writing on Foucault, aptly describes as an "audiovisual battle."[7]

This quote contains her entire comments on a theoretical approach to title design. And while her recognition that Michel Foucault's discussion of calligrams in *This is Not a Pipe* also provides a reference point for the current examination, her observations are not developed beyond what appears in this quotation. Her limited theoretical engagement has been repeated by a variety of film historians in surveys such as Fabio Carlini's history of title sequences, *Popcorn Time: L'arte dei titoli di testa* (in Italian). Some anthologies, such as *Das Buch zum Vorspann* (an anthology in German), approach film and television titles from a variety of critical, analytic perspectives. Other engagements with title sequences, notably Solange Landau's article "Das Intro als eigenständige Erzählform. Eine Typologie" from the *Journal of Serial Narration on Television*,[8] engages in a taxonomic identification of formal types of television show openers on American programs using the formalist approach common to design analysis and criticism. None of these articles or books develop a theory of the organization and semiotics specific to the composited text and imagery appearing in title sequences.

However, this absence of theories about typography or title design is not limited to the work of film historians and designers addressing their own fields: it is also strikingly absent within semiotics itself. Analyses such as those of Otto Neurath, Edward Tufte, or developed by Jacques Bertin's *Semiotics of Graphics* are formalist taxonomies describing iconic graphics and designs such as maps, yet they do not address typography beyond concerns with legibility. Nor does Umberto Eco's authoritative *A Theory of Semiotics* address the issues of typography at all, even though it thoroughly considers semiosis in a variety of forms and through a range of critical models. A particular consideration of either design or typography is conspicuously lacking from his study. To the extent that he addresses them, it is *en passant* as an implied extension of other comments about the organization and structure of semiotic protocols. This absence is not a weakness of Eco or Kepes or Rand or any of these historians and critics, but rather an omission that directs attention to the need for a particular consideration of not only typographic form, but its combination with other graphics and photography:

the composites of text–image that are essential to the identification and definition of title designs. The lack of theorization, and perhaps even the resistance to its proposal by designers, demonstrates what Eco described in *A Theory of Semiotics* as a *text-oriented* culture focused on identifying and emulating specific "models":

> There are cultures governed by a *system* of rules and there are cultures governed by a *repertoire* of texts imposing models of behavior. In the former category texts are generated by combinations of discrete units and are judged correct or incorrect according to their conformity to the combinational rules; in the latter category society directly generates texts, these constituting micro-units from which rules could be eventually be inferred, but that first and foremost propose models to be followed and imitated.[9]

The distinction or difference between *grammar-oriented* and *text-oriented* cultures Eco describes is recognizable in the role of "model texts" for design. The identification of elements through formalist analyses such as Bertin's theory masks an underlying disassociation of meaning from how the analysis proceeds: it is taxonomic, a classification system, not an account of how these classifications create meaning. Formalist analytics are actions a scientist capturing rare butterflies for further study might use to *begin* their research; however, design is not a butterfly, it is a cultural product serving specific meaningful ends and produced by humans, not emergent from some autonomous natural process. Ironically, for all their formalist analyses and claims to demonstrate general, abstract principles of design, these considerations revert to the specification of models to emulate—Eco's "repertoire of texts"—rather than the identification or proposal of a system of rules. This distinction is fundamental to Eco's proposal: grammar is not simply structure, but productive of meaning. The strictures posed by abstract principles do not in themselves produce the structure of language. This distinction repeats the separation of '*langue*' and '*parole*,' the distinction between combinatory rules and meaningful statements. The absence of such proposals from theories of typography become apparent when approaching works that are fundamentally a fusion of text and image, such as the motion picture title sequence.

Semiotics and Visual Form

The general absence of a theoretical foundation for typographics is compounded when confronting the complexity of type-image composites commonly appearing in both feature film and television title sequences. There is a minimal amount of semiotic theorization concerned with text and image relationships, primarily by Roland Barthes and Michel Foucault, both writing in the 1960s and 1970s, that provides some suggestive foundations for developing a more thorough semiotic analysis applicable to motion picture title sequences and the motion graphics field as a whole.

Barthes's discussion of the issues of denotation, connotation, and all their entangled complexities emerge through shifts between understanding images as visual forms and interpreting them as symbolic expressions. He described semiotic parallels between image and language in his analysis of the Mannerist painter Arcimboldo's use of metamorphic optical illusions to create shifts in the apparent contents of paintings where several different images coexist as potential recognitions within a single picture. Barthes's observations of Arcimboldo's multivalent works illuminate the application of semiotics to visual forms such as painting or motion pictures:

> Distance and proximity are promoters of meaning. Everything proceeds from spacing out or staggering of articulations. Meaning is born from a combination of non-signifying elements (phonemes, lines); but it is not sufficient to combine these elements to a first degree in order to exhaust the creation of meaning: what has been combined forms aggregates which can combine again among themselves a second, a third time.[10]

Individual parts of the image function as elements whose combination produces meaning, whether it is a recognition of form, or advancing into greater complexity as the arrangement of "signs"—language—resulting in a particular and "precise" statement. The shifting levels Barthes identifies as an explicit feature of Arcimboldo's work corresponds to the movement between distinct recognitions of imagery *in* the painting and their transition from those depictions to become symbolic, suggesting allegorical interpretations. These changes in perception are connected to the level adopted in considering the painting's "apparent" contents:

> It is by an effort of distance, by changing the level of perception, that I receive another message, a hyper-metropic apparatus which, like a decoding grid, allows me suddenly to perceive the total meaning, the "real" meaning. Thus Arcimboldo imposes a system of substitution . . . and, in the same way a system of transposition.[11]

The conscious choice of the observer in *how* to look at a composite head by Arcimboldo determines *which* portion of that image appears as a component—for example, a "nose"—and *what* the relationship between those components may be—the formation of a face, or the "disintegration" into other forms. Or again, the interpretation becomes a stage in a complex shift to another level of consideration as when, for example, the head in question is identified as "Vertumnus" [God of the Bountiful Harvest], an allegorical figure that also happens to be a portrait of Arcimboldo's patron, Emperor Rudolf II. The transition from various, immanent recognitions—a peach, a cheek—to higher-level interpretations such as the allegorical meaning of this portrait head depends on externalities that are outside or beyond the image itself. This turning away from depiction into the connotation of the image is a specific deployment of the viewer's established fluency and expertise rather than their lower-level capacities of recognition at "play" in identifying the shifting imagery within the painting itself.

The higher-level recognitions Barthes identifies cannot be readily contained by taxonomic analyses. Formalist approaches are ill-equipped to address the complex shifts of meaning within images-in-themselves; once combined with typography, this difficulty only becomes more pronounced. Considering the complexity of images-in-themselves demonstrates the need for semiotic approaches to title design by making the roles of imagery and its synchronization with sound/music in proposing meaning obvious; the addition of typography transforms these lower-level considerations. Understanding this audio-visual foundation's relationship to semiotics without the mediating effects of typography enables the dynamic created by its addition to emerge clearly.

The relevance of Surrealist art for exactly this type of theoretical consideration is not usual, as art historian Dawn Ades observes in her introduction to the study *Dali's Optical Illusions*:

> Modernism in art is concerned with the abstract, the formal, the conceptual, and the pure material object. Surrealism alone has systematically sought the interface between internal and external realities, illusion and vision, perception and thought.[12]

The connections between perception and thought align with the distinctions between denotation and connotation: denotation seemingly presents us with the thing itself, only connotation makes the link with thought an accessible dimension of the visual work. In shifting from immediacy of encounter to interpreted meaning, the audience is invited to deploy not just their capacities for shifting between lower-level recognitions and higher-level order, but to engage these images as paralinguistic constructs organized through connotations of absent subjects evoked in a chain of recognitions that are strictly denotative. Barthes explains these shifts as rhetoric-rendered-visual, results that are specifically an 'optical poetry' adapting familiar verbal devices in its construction:

> Arcimboldo exploits the "curiosities" of language, plays on synonymy and homonymy. His painting has a linguistic basis, his imagination is, strictly speaking, poetic: it does not create signs, it combines them, permutes them, deflects them—precisely what the practitioner of language does.[13]

His concern is the extension of established protocols of verbal/textual semiosis to what are purely and innately visual constructions. Making this connection allows for a consideration of images as semiotic forms in themselves. The parallels between language activities and visual experiences he draws in Arcimboldo's work are compelling because these particular images *do* engage with complex shifts of interpretation that move fluidly between foundational recognitions—brush strokes and smears of color—into multiple levels of strictly denotative content—fruits and faces. The analogies set up between arrangements such as peach/cheek translate verbal comparisons into visual terms—revealing paralinguistic meanings. This joining of visual and textual allows for considerations of both elements as part of a singular semiotic theory.

However, while these structures are easily comprehended in painting since it is a pure artifact, autonomously constructed; their relevance for photography or motion pictures made with live actors is less immediately apparent. The applicability of Barthes's observations about the paralinguistic functions of images to photography and motion pictures can be demonstrated by considering a single shot from *The House on Skull Mountain* (1974) that features a metamorphic illusion similar to those of Arcimboldo. It provides a case study for how semiotic approaches can be applied to the denotative imagery of photography. This shot was chosen for analysis precisely because it allows a focus on the imagistic *without* the typography common to title designs. The issues revealed in this analysis of visual composites synchronized with sound are identical to those faced by title designs, allowing an understanding of how semiotic approaches can be applied to motion pictures that can then be extended to an analysis of text–image composites.

Although this shot [Figure 1.1, left] is atypical of what appears in *The House on Skull Mountain*,[14] its structure and organization parallels the effects created by Arcimboldo's paintings, but adapted to the temporal development of a motion picture: it begins as a medium shot of a woman ("Lorena Christophe," played by Janee Michelle) looking off screen to the left, her hand at her mouth; the initial framing hides the double image it contains. As the shot pulls back, it gradually reveals she is sitting at a dressing stand, and the composition makes its duplicity apparent—the scene has been carefully arranged to create a double image where the curve of the mirror is the top of a skull and the woman's dark hair provide the eye sockets. This second image becomes progressively more obvious, until once the camera move ends, a white skull shape appears superimposed over this composition, asserting the optical illusion's priority. This shot is a quotation of nineteenth century illustrator C. Allen Gilbert's metamorphic illusion *All is Vanity* (published by House of Art, 1892) [Figure 1.1, right]. The role of this quotation in proposing an expanded meaning for this shot reveals the mediating effects the audience's past experiences and knowledge have on the construction of their interpretations—the same issues required for meaning in written/verbal text (the knowledge that enables a reader to understand what typography says)—emerge in this purely visual quotation.

Both shot and illustration are 'reflections' of each other; Honthaner's quotation transposes Gilbert's composition so it is reversed, as if seen in a mirror, even though the arrangement of individual elements in the images remains constant: the burning candle, the bottles/teeth arrayed before the circle of the mirror, the woman's slightly raised hand, touching her face. Because the shot is photographic, it lacks the lowest level of material construction common to all paintings, but develops the same composite effects created by shifting denotative contents between woman/skull.

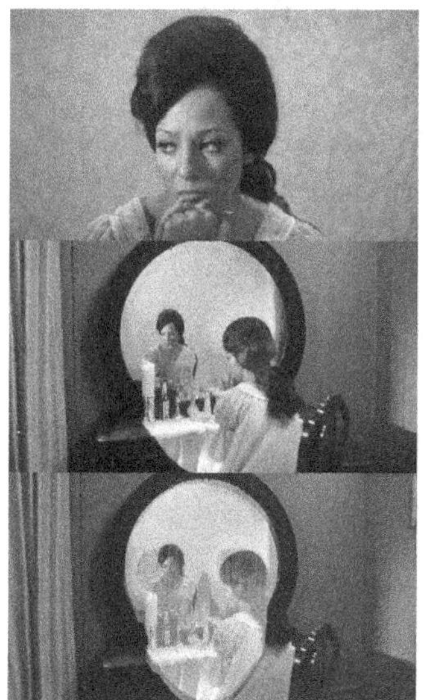

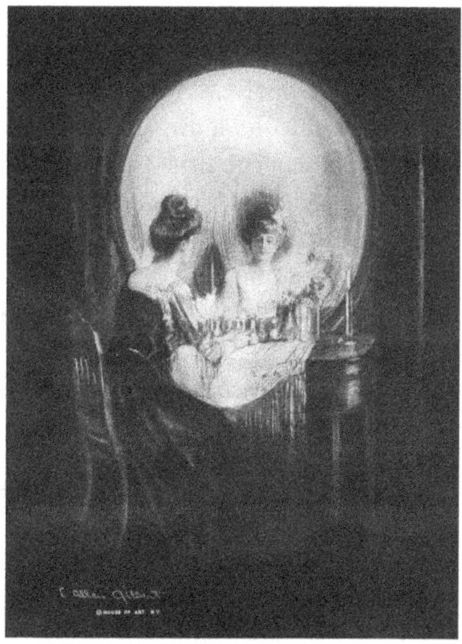

Figure 1.1 Metamorphic illusion of woman at vanity/skull
LEFT: stills from *The House on Skull Mountain* (1974)
RIGHT: *All is Vanity* by C. Allen Gilbert (House of Art, 1892)

However, there are a number of differences between the source of this illusion and its quotation in *The House on Skull Mountain*: in the original image, the woman directly addresses the picture's audience, seemingly meeting their gaze, while in the restaging, she looks away, apparently unaware of the camera filming. Gilbert's woman looks like a classic "Gibson girl"—a stereotypical image of wealthy, white American 'aristocracy'—common to illustrations of the 1890s, while in the film she is a contemporary 'office girl'—someone who works for a living; she is also black. They are different, yet the denotative contents Barthes's analysis identifies as the first level of analysis remain recognizably constant. The reversals of illustration/shot are not an accident, but part of a systematic series of reversals and doublings running throughout the film that present a fantasy of the death of racism, summarized by the metonymic relationship of film quotation to original illustration. The plot is set in motion by events surrounding a rich, black, "Haitian" family attending the reading of the matriarch's will at the family mansion outside Atlanta, Georgia. But this fantasy is belied by the plot itself where a visibly white man who is supposed to be a "mixed-race" cousin ("Dr. Andrew Cunningham" played by Victor French) must save his black cousin ("Lorena Christophe," played by Janee Michelle, who appears in this shot) from the horrors of voodoo and the superstitious magic that is part of their Haitian heritage: she must be liberated from her origins—her *black* past.

In 1892, any black woman, were she present to Gilbert's image, is (literally) invisible: her role would have been as a servant, doing the bidding of her white mistress whose presentation has a slightly moralizing tone in this optical illusion: it is a classic *vanitas* rendered simultaneously as *momento mori*. The title *All is Vanity* is thus redundant with the other iconography contained in/as the image itself: the burning candle alludes to time passing (beauty is fleeting) coupled with the intensity of her gaze outwards at the audience, engaging, challenging the viewer to acknowledge that she *is* beautiful—a beauty that is artificially created by the bottles arrayed before her, an illusion.

Simultaneously, her beauty on display assumes the form of a skull: the circle of her mirror is also its curved edge; her flowing, sensuous dark hair the black pits of eye sockets that leer vacantly; the perfumes and potions of her bottles, the distended roots of teeth without gums. Within her beauty lies the unmistakable image of death. Michel Foucault's theorization of vision as an ordering and dominating model of knowledge and understanding provides a foundation for exploring those peculiar semiotics wherein language collapses into image, and the photograph ceases to be purely denotative and becomes a sign in a larger rhetorical complex. Vision, as he theorizes it, sets in motion these shifting engagements of connotation and denotation: these paired and mutually exclusive images are also linked. The traditional conjunction of skull (Death) with youth and beauty lies within the *inherent* structure of both *vanitas* and *momento mori* as iconographic systems of death-within-beauty that is specific to the *vanitas* and finds specific demonstration in this metamorphic image. The dimensions of *momento mori* are superseded by the organization of Gilbert's *vanitas*. Crafting the double image in this fashion invokes a morality play, where the instantaneous transformation into a leering skull critiques both her vanity and her unwavering gaze (the woman's direct address of the viewer)—her reflection meets the gaze of her audience, iconographically a standard element in the *vanitas* picture. Foucault's theorizing of a materialist understanding of the visible world organized and ordered through visional dominance that equates seeing with knowledge, and is embodied precisely in metaphors of vision as understanding, what Foucault terms the "empirical gaze" in *The Birth of the Clinic*:

> seeing consists in leaving to experience its greatest corporeal opacity; the solidity, the obscurity, the density of things closed in upon themselves, have powers of truth that they owe not to light, but to the slowness of the gaze that passes over them, around them, and gradually into them, bringing them nothing more than its own light. The residence of truth in the dark center of things is linked, paradoxically, to this sovereign power of *the empirical gaze* that turns their darkness into light.[15]

His conception of vision presents sight as an operative paradigm for comprehension directly linked to the physical body rather than a transcendent, metaphysical knowledge. Gilbert's metamorphic image invokes an uncomfortable shifting of positions around her gaze outwards to the audience. It is this woman's self-possession (apparent in the even gaze she directs at the viewer) which comes under assault in Gilbert's painting—the illusion of youth, the beauty she presents, is simultaneously an *act* that hides death: "beauty inevitably fades" is the moralizing message delivered against her self-assured presentation to onlooker via mirror. It is the act of "seeing" that produces recognition, becomes identified with knowing because of its central place in the creation of that comprehension of visual experience as knowledge contained by language; this is the relationship of *telling::showing*. Seeing thus comes to dominate what is seen; observation is a mode of gaining power over the observed.

The contrast between the metamorphic image in *The House on Skull Mountain* and Gilbert's original could not be stronger. The development of this shot is significant. In place of the self-assured, self-conscious woman who has already composed herself and addresses the viewer with her gaze, in *The House on Skull Mountain* her counterpart is an uncertain, perhaps even frightened woman who gazes vacantly at a space insistently outside the audience's view; her gaze does not engage the viewer. She first appears in close-up, and while it is obvious she is thinking about something (reflecting), it is not immediately apparent that she is *literally* shown in reflection—that what the audience sees is her visage reflected by a dressing stand mirror. This fact emerges as the shot pulls back, away from her, in the process 'discovering' the double image (emergent skull) whose presence is emphasized by a synchronized musical cue and superimposed white skull shape. While the same classic elements of the *vanitas* are present—the woman's reflection in the mirror, the burning candle, that appear in Gilbert's painting—this is not a *vanitas*, but rather only a *momento mori*, one that invokes the *vanitas* even as it denies the role of vanity in this invocation of death. Where Gilbert's image is a moralizing statement about fading beauty and the self-imposed illusions employed to hide it, the double image in *The House on Skull Mountain* reveals a lurking death, an omnipresent yet invisible threat inherent to this scene rendered via the soundtrack as pounding voodoo drums and atonal screech as the superimposed skull form appears; the death thus invoked is not her vanity, but her race, that of her blackness. The reversal of relationships between *All is Vanity* and *The House on Skull Mountain*—the transformations of *vanitas/momento mori*, reversed composition, and race—are reflective of the larger social transformations and inversions that run throughout the film; these transfers are all indicators of the superstitious magic that assails this woman because of her Haitian heritage.

The shift in her gaze from direct address (illustration) to insistent disconnection (film)—not just a reflection of cinematic convention where the actor pretends the camera is not present—also serves to interiorize the woman at the mirror because she is clearly looking *at* something, but *what* is unknown as it lies outside the frame, invisible within this shot and physically never revealed by the context within the film. This unknown "object" in *The House on Skull Mountain* is clearly troubling her, consuming her thoughts, and its absence from the audience's view forces a consideration that the *what* could easily be the skull that emerges from the composition's duplicity. The superimposition thus assumes a rhetorical role, present for the audience as an assertion of the double image, but one that is invisible to Lorena, who is so essential to its appearance. This emergent form—the death's head—is not a part of the scene, but rather a reflection upon it, potentially a visualization of the character's thoughts—evoked by the voodoo drums—graphically on-screen in a way that is both inherently a part of the action (emergent from the composition itself) and a presentation of what is not (cannot be) shown on-screen: Lorena's thoughts—her fear, signified by the voodoo drums, becoming manifest as the superimposed skull. By combining the metamorphic image with the secondary assertion of *momento mori* via superimposition, the only conclusion possible is that she is thinking about death—about how fleeting life is, that beauty always fades, that there is never enough time. But the 'death' in this film is also linked to the superstitious magic of voodoo, fundamentally connected to the 'blackness' of the family. The only character *not* subject to this specific appeal is the white man (the hero, Dr. Andrew Cunningham) who must rescue the black woman (the heroine, Lorena Christophe) from the destructive death-magic of Haitian voodoo.

However, the evocation of this underlying rhetorical meaning concerned with race relations in the United States, allegorical in nature, can only be accessed through a different lexicon of recognitions, cultural rather than perceptual-visual. This complexity of relationship between quotation and immanent image is precisely the point: the meaning of this sequence, while accentuated by the soundtrack and reinforced by the superimposed image of a skull, fundamentally requires the audience to understand and identify the quotation that organizes this image. The use of this reference in developing the rhetorical aspects of this shot transforms the visual materials into a language; this action is more common in title sequences, an effect produced not by the visual materials, but through the use of typography. The emergent meaning of this shot is *not* the denoted meaning of recognized imagery. These movements beyond the constraints of the image are what Barthes called the "third meaning" in his discussion of Arcimboldo. Meaning emergent not from recognition but in the connection and association with absent-from-depiction factors; in connotation one finds the linkages provided by cultural associations and the emergent meanings provided by strictly historical context:

> Quite different is the third meaning, the allegorical meaning: in order to read here the head of *Summer* or of *Calvin*, I require a metonymic culture, which makes me associate certain fruits (and not others) with Summer, or, more subtly still, the austere ugliness of a face with Calvinist puritanism; and as soon as we leave the dictionary of words for a chart of cultural meanings, of associations of ideas, in short for an encyclopedia of received ideas, we enter into the infinite realm of connotations.[16]

The rhetoric of race depends on the quotation. It is embedded in this shot in *The House on Skull Mountain* and articulated through a specific pattern of reiteration and reversal apparent in the differences between historical illustration and filmic shot, but can only be identified by how these elements align with the cultural and historical particulars these elements connote. Simply recognizing the quotation is insufficient for the development of its meaning. This specific collection of linkages and transfers organizes the development of the double image in *The House on Skull Mountain*, apparent through both superimposed skull and accompanying soundtrack. The differences with Gilbert's image are therefore of great significance—the shift in race and deflection of the gaze—indicating the most apparent difference, her race, may also be the reason the death motif is not just an optical construction (the metamorphic nature of the image), but is also asserted through the superimposed white form. The linkage of white form to death, invoked by the voodoo drums, is an acknowledgment of the subtext to the whole film: an *imaginary* death to racism. Specific details from the story are organized around this fantasy: the house is an antebellum plantation manor, located in the outskirts of Atlanta, Georgia, a state notorious for its opposition to racial integration in the 1950s and 1960s. That the family is Haitian, rather than American, descendants of a former French colony that also achieved freedom from European rule following a bloody revolutionary war—this choice is not accidental given the similarities between both countries' origins—nevertheless has a specific difference: in Haiti, the revolutionaries were black slaves from Africa, rather than white, Euro-descended slave owners.

The death phantom that appears at the end of this shot being specifically white is thus significant: not just because skulls are white, but also because the question of race ("whiteness/blackness") haunts the film as a whole. The reversal of relationships from Gilbert's *All is Vanity* to *The House on Skull Mountain* is not simply a transposition accommodating the film's black actress, but a simultaneous (doubled) implication that ascending in social status requires the rejection of her Haitian origins (her 'blackness').

The doubling of "doctors" in the film repeats the same doublings of white-black that appear in this shot: the threat posed by voodoo is embodied in the "witch doctor" who is the *black* villain, defeated by the *white* doctor. The linkage of (white) skull with (black) voodoo drums further dramatizes the conflict between superstition (black, Haitian heritage) and the rationality embodied in the white protagonist that ultimately prevails: the superstition is simultaneously a figure of death (the skull), and will (symbolically) die by being made white—the white form, in asserting itself as a symbol of death also obscures the black woman, transforming her into the skull, eliminating her with its whiteness—as the doubled image becomes visually dominant.

The figure of death that appears within Gilbert's image—the metonymy between arrangement and skull—is absent from the reversed composition, yet informs and structures these reversals: while both are examples of *momento mori*, the remembrance of death has a different signification in both pictures, a difference that emerges precisely through the shift in gaze. In *The House on Skull Mountain*, Lorena gazes away, off screen, at something *other* than the viewer. The subject of her gaze, a fearful contemplation, can only be the threat posed by the racial subtext of the film itself: her Haitian heritage (blackness) that is appearing, insistently, throughout the film and which can literally be heard on the soundtrack (even though this musical cue is conventionally understood by the audience to be non-diegetic, unheard by the characters on-screen). Pounding in the background is a dark, irrational, superstitious force that is inseparable from American pop cultural ideas of Haiti: not simply black, but foreign, *other*. This connection of the death-figure to her heritage belies the surface level of the film's premise, that of a rich black Haitian family whose matriarch has died and whose heirs have gathered to hear the will, instead transforming that *surface* into the horror itself: the horror of the black other, rendered visible in this singular shot whose transformations and reiterations of Gilbert's picture bring these themes into focus. The danger posed by voodoo is not the supernatural threat common to horror films—it is instead the horror posed by the discovery of *blackness* represented by voodoo as the sweaty, rhythmic, superstitious primitive: beneath the superficial fantasy of a dissolution and banishment of racism lies, instead, a fundamentally racist conception of both white and black, one where the "Haitian" serves to represent the dangerous, threatening, and irrational other to American (white) rationality.

This conversion from imagistic denotation to allegorical connotation requires the audience to impose a series of lexia—first denotative, then associative (the recognitions of quotation and reiteration), and finally strictly cultural—in order to produce an interpretation of this short filmed sequence as representative of the whole film's signification. To see the whole in the fragment—synecdoche—is to impose a holographic ordering that aligns the various elements in a hierarchy where the interpretation emerges as a logical, even natural, conclusion. The fluid movement between different levels of interpretation shifts comprehension and engagement while the fundamental material remains constant: these dynamics become important for text–image composites—the shifts in second-level interpretations surrounding the rebus mode develop from lower-level distinctions established in the figure–ground and calligram modes.

Traditional Conceptions of Title Sequences

In place of a robust theory of title sequences and their organization-design are a variety of "traditions" about the role of the titles in relation to the main production. These understandings have developed because the title sequence has been a common element in the presentation of motion pictures throughout their history in the United States; but, as noted earlier, this history is one that has *not* received sustained theoretical attention. The organization of title sequences has varied greatly in complexity, duration, and distinguishability from the central drama over the more than 125 years of motion picture production in the United States; the earliest examples were produced by Edison's Black Maria studio in the 1890s. These title sequences were minimal, a simple title card that served as a unique identifier for purposes of copyright registry; however, with the shift to dramatic, feature-length narratives in the 1910s, the need for text on-screen became increasingly necessary to present dialogue and other narrative information.

The importance of these title cards—both for the main title and dispersed throughout the film as intertitles—gave their designer/writers a prominence during the so-called "silent era" before the dominance of synchronous sound productions they will lose once sync sound production begins after 1927. These designers who received on-screen credit for their work differed dramatically from the Modernist style introduced by Saul Bass in the 1950s—their work was highly limited technologically compared to those later titles which used an optical printer to combine live action and graphics. Unlike the titles/credits from the beginning of the "talkies" in the later 1920s and 1930s, these "silent" titles were an integral part of the narrative itself, providing not only the absent dialogue, but presenting editorial commentary and exposition. These earlier designs were most commonly produced as static title cards, and the distinction between expository and other credits in one of the films produced without a synchronized soundtrack was often oblique, if apparent at all.

Ferdinand Penney Earle's work with "Art Title Design" that received on-screen credit in *Daddy Long Legs* (1919) is typical, appearing throughout the film to provide narrative exposition. These title cards are an exemplar of the approach common to this early period that renders them comparable to what appears in a picture book or illustrated magazine of the 1910s or 1920s [Figure 1.2]. Individual title cards combine typography and painting and then are toned various hues—blue, sepia, magenta, or green—a design choice that reflects the emotional tenor of the text on that title card. The opening credits and initial explosion use these hues to group different series of titles: blue for the three opening credit title cards, then magenta for the start of the exposition. Once sound production begins, these decorative arrangements of text and image will be confined to the opening credits, and the designer's role in their production will rapidly fade. The transition from "silent" to "talkie" production is apparent in the disappearance of the identified title designer from the opening credit sequence. Jack Jarmuth receives on-screen credit for his work in 1927's *The Jazz Singer*, but by 1934 such on-screen design credits will disappear.

The return to giving on-screen credit to title designers, starting with Saul Bass in 1954 (for *Carmen Jones*) and more notably on *The Man with the Golden Arm* (1955) [Figure 1.3], happened in context with graphic designers

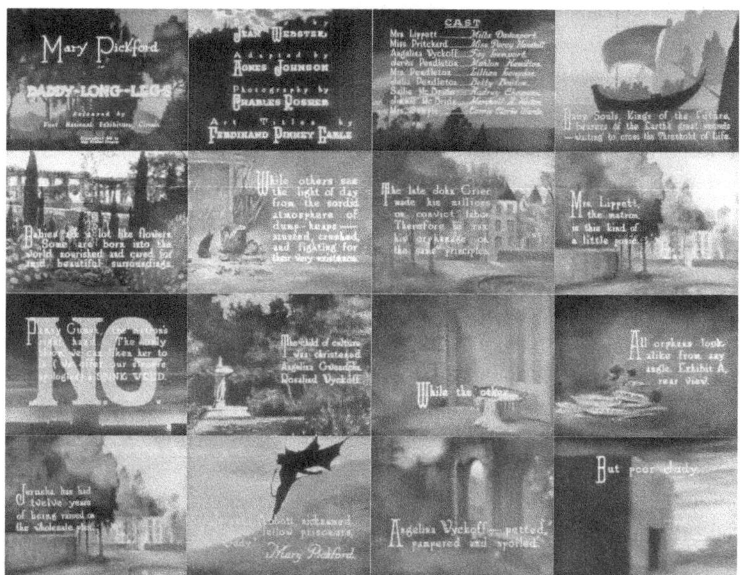

Figure 1.2 "Art Title Cards" by Ferdinand Pinney Earle from the first five minutes of *Daddy Long Legs* (First National, 1919); there is no clear demarcation between title cards used in the opening sequence design and later narrative intertitles

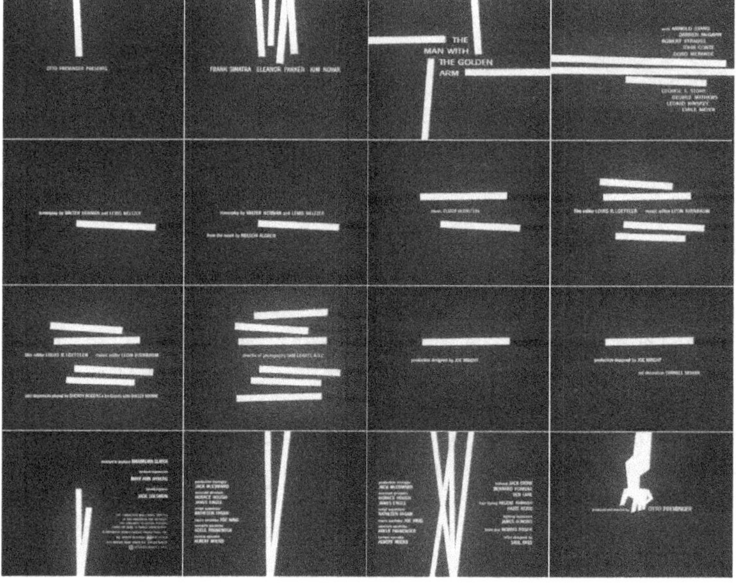

Figure 1.3 All the title cards in *The Man with the Golden Arm* (1955), showing Saul Bass's Modernist design of the sequence

such as Alvin Lustig and Paul Rand actually including their *signature* as an essential compositional feature of their designs. Like the signature in graphic design, on-screen credit as a "title designer" is a feature of how the important, serious Modern title designers such as Saul Bass, Maurice Binder, Robert Brownjohn or Pablo Ferro identified and distinguished their work as different from the (often uncredited) work of designers working in the studios, or at independent 'optical' companies such as *The Pacific Art and Title Company*, better known as "Pacific Title."[17]

This mid-century shift from uncredited, anonymous production work, to credited, high-profile marker for both seriousness of aesthetic intent and signifier of prestige production came as a sudden transformation—even though it was prepared for by more than a decade's worth of graphic designers in the United States boldly signing their designs.[18] Following Saul Bass's very limited theorizing of the title sequence in his own work,[19] these designs are commonly understood as a transition signaling movement into the diegetic space of the film: they function as an invocation of a "magic circle" for storytelling.[20] Bass discussed this role for title sequences in an interview shortly before his death in 1996 with historian Pamela Haskin:

> My initial thoughts about what a title could do was to set the mood and to prime the underlying core of the film's story; to express the story in some metaphorical way. I saw the title as a way of conditioning the audience, so that when the film actually began, viewers would already have an emotional resonance with it.[21]

Bass's description of titles as an introduction to the narrative space is typical of designer's conceptions of title sequences. Because they are commonly situated at the very beginning of the film, theorizing them as a transition between the reality 'outside' the narrative and the fictional world 'inside' (i.e., as paratext) seems logical. The audience's simultaneous awareness that the actors are posing as someone other than who they are organizes the entire process of the film, not simply those of the titles, but the fiction itself. Title sequences are wholly subservient to the production that follows: because the titles occupy the space *between* the actions of the fictional story (the diegesis) and the reality that lies outside that artificial (imaginary) space, however much the rest of the film might resemble a documentary presentation of 'reality,' for the paratextual understanding, the title sequence is a "gateway" between these mutually present, contradictory relationships.

Bass's role in promoting this conception of the opening title sequence is self-serving: it provides a justification for his receiving on-screen credit within the sequence itself (and supports the high rates he charged to design and produce these sequences). This view of the title sequence as a synecdotal encapsulation of the narrative itself, whether in graphic form (as in Bass's 1955 design for *The Man with the Golden Arm*[22]) or through the symbolic evocations of montage is commonly linked to their conception and interpretation. As Georg Stanitzek explains in his article "Reading the Title Sequence," the film is begun paradoxically *with* and *after* the title sequence:

> Title sequences create a divided focus of attention, the separation of the inside from the outside, of what is the play of the narrative from what is documenting the production, cinematic narrative from film commentary, intradiegetic from extradiegetic information. The title sequence achieves this as a film within a film, in that it introduces, in that it—semi-autonomously—establishes itself as distinct from the main film. [. . .] It is in this sense that the title sequence constitutes the beginning of the film, which, at the same time, it represents. As the beginning, the title sequence sets itself apart in a particular way; namely, insofar as it is endowed with its own beginning and end, it establishes itself as distinct and develops its own coherence. In turn, its own beginning might possibly be seen as set apart; as a rule, the title sequence starts with the studio's or the distributor's trademark logo, which itself acts as a kind of title to the title sequence proper as the title sequence does to the movie proper.[23]

For such an introductory role/purpose, almost any design might work equally well so long as it sufficiently serves to prepare the audience for the story that follows. To designate the transition between everyday life and the cinematic experience as the role of the title sequence inherently recreates a specific set of inherited conventions from earlier forms of theater; it plays the role of the theatrical curtain, parting as the program begins, and closing once the performance has concluded. Any particularly notable features in any title sequence are thus simply the flourishes that might be expected of any well designed textile: decorative, interesting, belonging to a tradition of earlier designs, but of only limited significance in themselves. Critical considerations and analysis of these designs thus become exercises in stylistic affirmation: clarifying traditions, identifying the precedents, elaborating upon the embellishments provided by the titles—all that can be expected of what is essentially a minor art. Yet what is of interest about this often neglected form is precisely the ways that it has an ambiguous relationship to the motion picture that follows: what role does the title sequence have for this, the main focus of so much theory, criticism, and historical analysis? For much of the history of motion pictures made in Hollywood, the designers responsible for the titles went uncredited, their skills and work passing in front of the audience often without comment or consideration by the viewers—and yet this opening moment (so often invisible to criticism and analysis) is the *actual* beginning of the motion picture itself.

As film historian Georg Stanitzek notes, title sequences *are* produced in a secondary relation to the main part of the motion picture;[24] however, they are also created independently of that production, employing an entirely different crew and using procedures more commonly used in sign painting and animated cartoons; however, this division of labor into discrete tasks performed by specialists has been a feature of the Hollywood studio system since its inception: the producer, the director, the cinematographer, the screenwriter are seldom the same person. The musical score composed for the film or television show bears many of the same constraints and distance from the rest of the production that the titles do, yet the title sequence has been singularly distanced from the rest of the production process.

This distancing of the title sequence—as subservient and at the same time independent of the rest of the motion picture—suggests a paradoxical role for these beginnings (and sometimes endings) for movies. To be subservient implies the subordination of the constructive and aesthetic form of the titles to the design and structure of the main 'body' of narration and production that follows. And while the title sequence's content—the names and other credits that appear—are deeply dependent on the specifics of the film production to which a particular title sequence is attached, at the same time, the form of these titles may not resemble the film that follows in any fashion at all, aside from what can be heard in the music composed as the theme. The visual form can be and often is entirely independent of what appears *inside* the actual production.

The Image–Animation Problem

As the design, running time, and quantity of title cards increased in the early years of the twentieth century as the motion picture industry developed, individual films also started to credit both the production personnel and actors who appeared in the film; the design and quantity of title cards increased; complex mixtures of animation and optical effects were common by the end of the 1920s. It is this hybrid beginning where animation, graphics, and live action cinematography combined that invokes contemporary concerns with the *nature* of motion pictures, what has been called "the image–animation problem." Early in the history of motion pictures, animation was marginalized as secondary to the consideration and production of live action films and the mechanics of realism accompanying those productions. In the process, visual effects and motion graphics (such as title sequences) were either ignored or elided from the consideration of cinema as an institutional practice focused on the creation of live action narrative-fictional dramas.

A range of contemporary film historians and theorists such as André Gaudreault, Philippe Marion, and Alan Cholodenko, as well as new media theorists such as Lev Manovich, have brought attention to the hybrid nature of live action/animation that have become commonplace in digital practice. This problem is critical rather than technological—a reflection of shifting productive and exhibition technologies from celluloid to digital video accompanied by novel integrations of live action and animation such as using motion capture to animate digital "puppets" that are highly detailed and photorealistic, yet at the same time entirely artificial. These intersections between using live actors and animation only become a problem when considered in relation to the dominant conception of "cinema" as reflecting a link between an originary action performed live in front of a camera and its mediated appearance in the finished motion picture. For such an understanding of "cinema," digital hybrids where live actors become model-controllers for animations rendered by a computer, fully replacing the live action performance with synthetic animations, can be nothing other than an existential challenge; thus, the "image–animation problem" is an identity crisis for historical conceptions of "cinema."

These issues are problems of understanding motion pictures via *depiction* versus *denotation*: it is tempting to look at the photograph (even in the form of a digital image) and assume a direct connection between what is depicted and what was present in front of the camera. This historical link of photography to denotation is innate. Photography has developed around this supposed direct translation, and from its historical basis in photo-chemical emulsions and light sensitivity, motion pictures have also employed this same connection as a foundational moment in the understanding of the medium as such. It is a relational conception of photography (and cinema) that Barthes explains in his book *Camera Lucida*:

> The Photograph does not necessarily say *what is no longer*, but only and for certain *what has been*. This distinction is decisive. In front of a photograph, our consciousness does not necessarily take the nostalgic path of memory (how many photographs are outside of individual time), but for every photograph existing in the world, the path of certainty: the Photograph's existence is to ratify what it represents.[25]

Barthes equates the photographic image with denotation: it is the thing itself shown, utterly specific and individuated, recognized not by its similarity to other things, but by being itself. The exigencies of mimesis and construction give way to the reality of the depicted thing as a "proof" of its presence in the world. This understanding of photographs reaches an apogee with the realism of the cinematic image, and the tendency to claim as André Bazin does in "The Ontology of the Photographic Image" that "we are obliged to believe in the existence of the object represented: it is truly re-presented, made present in time and space."[26] While it might be tempting to dismiss these comments as naiveté, they reflect the immediate sense of photography as comingling the actions of depiction and denotation—that the image is a cipher that brings what it depicts immediately into consciousness in a way that the always-constructed images of drawings and other graphic arts do not. The generated image produced by digital systems complicates this immediate sense of presence by simulating the reality of traditional photographs completely. The audience's tendency to confuse the depiction with denotation renders these images *as* what they appear to be, whether they *actually* are or not; both Barthes and Bazin make the same point about photography's apparent reality.

Animated and live action elements are often comingled in title sequences; their integration is not only as superimposed/composited typography, but have been linked in more fundamental ways, allowing a modulation of live action into animation and vice versa. Walter Lantz, who contracted with Universal starting in 1935 to produce animated graphics and is best known for creating Woody Woodpecker, is uncredited for *My Man Godfrey* (Universal, 1936).[27] His design demonstrates this entanglement clearly as both a function of the design's significance and its technical production: organized as a continuous pan across matte painting buildings of an imaginary Manhattan where the credits are literally set in lights that reflect on the East river, this singular "shot" gradually begins to include smaller, darker hovels of a 'Hooverville' built under the Brooklyn Bridge [Figure 1.4]. Everything in this opening sequence is a graphic until it reaches the end and the painting comes to life as the first live action shot of the film. The transition is seamless, looking like nothing more than an intensification of the animated title to become live action. This entanglement does not invalidate the image–animation problem; neither does it alter the underlying challenge addressed by the digital system's transformation of photoreal imagery from a rigid and difficult-to-manipulate material into one that fluidly blends animated and simulated elements with actual photography. Animation has always been a foundational aspect of motion pictures. The complex systems of editing, photography, and assembly employed in visual effects and

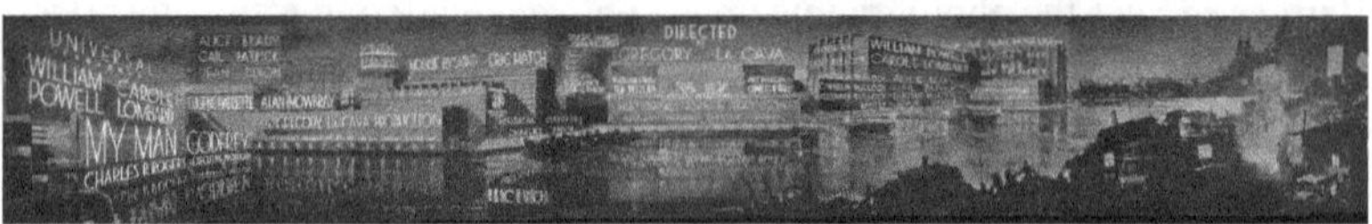

Figure 1.4 Composite panorama, *My Man Godfrey* (Universal, 1936)

motion graphics—even before the emergence of digital systems—function only because of an underlying, shared foundation as animated still imagery. Much earlier technologies than contemporary computer systems also invoked these issues, but with less insistence and frequency than contemporary digital animation and compositing now do.

Optical printing is the most apparent of these historical technologies, invented in 1929 by cinematographer Linwood Dunn, who would employ its capacities with seamlessly transforming live action footage on Orson Welles's 1941 film *Citizen Kane*.[28] This technical refinement over earlier compositing machines, such as the projection printer, allowed greater control and precision in the compositing of filmed material, especially with its particular capacities for compositing imagery, thus allowing both the creation of visual effects employing miniatures and the combination of complex animation with typography. Because optical printing is fundamentally a process of rephotography, the materials being optically printed can be subjected to a range of transformations that affect the image as a whole, as well as its motion, duration, and contents. The approach to imaging that optical printing suggests can be readily transferred and adapted for use with digital technology precisely because digital approaches were developed as a way to create optical printer effects without the time and expense of actually using an optical printer.

Optical printing enabled the production of radically new kinds of visual imagery in motion because it is based on rephotography and enables the systematic combination of different materials using a technique similar to stop motion animation. The technical "revolution" of digital technology is not a transformation of earlier, analog capacities for optical printing, but an improvement in their efficiency and reduction in cost. Film historian Raymond Fielding's monograph on visual effects and composite photography, *The Technique of Special Effects Cinematography*, concludes with a discussion of the future prospects of the then-emerging digital computer:

> There is no question that the introduction and perfection of an electronic optical printer could theoretically revolutionize the process of composite cinematography and optical printing. In addition to all of the capabilities of a modern optical printer, such a system could be able to enhance photographic images, minimize grain, add color to black-and-white images or alter colors radically, multiply image elements to whatever extent desired, correct over- and under-exposure, and remove scratches or wires from within the picture area. It is even theoretically possible that such a device could separate designated foreground details out of the background without the need for blue-screen backings, and that computer software could be designed to accomplish

> this, more-or-less automatically, with a minimum of human instruction. With such a system, the images of expensive miniatures, set pieces, props, crowds, water and sky scenes, and the like might be 'stockpiled' and retrieved at will for use in new films! In theory, at least, all things are possible with such a system.[29]

The hypothetical system Fielding describes in 1984 is now a commonplace technology, having fully replaced the labor intensive practice of precision masking and rephotography with faster, cheaper, and seamless digital imaging that accomplishes all the imagined tasks he describes. This uniformity is important; establishing a continuous line of approach across the seemingly vast technical gulf between analog and digital technologies renders the issues of mechanical production irrelevant to the organizing principles and conventions employed in the creation of any particular design. The shifts between one technology and another can be ignored. Their impacts are on ease of production and how common we can anticipate any particular use might be, but does not impact the meaning-producing structures or their role in maintaining a social order that prioritizes vision and narrative.

The image–animation problem, with its underlying focus on technical mechanics, reaffirms the supposition that analog and digital technologies are antithetical, requiring a foundational reassessment. The problems of *depiction* versus *denotation* that produce the image–animation problem for cinema studies is the same set of issues that lead graphic design to construct its elaborate taxonomic histories: the organization of visual material confuses denotation for depiction—the arrangement is the arrangement—subject to the rules and codes of composition, creating the illusion that a careful study of the parts will lead to an understanding of the denotative meaning and its connotative associations. The blending of depictive and denotative understandings in historical photography/cinematography and the model exemplars that inform these studies ratify the established hierarchies of value and importance. A concern with the forms that these ingrained values marginalize reveals the continuous interplay between mimesis and its ontological link to an external reality—precisely the issues of vision and knowledge that inform Foucault's and Barthes's criticism of images.

In the title sequence and motion graphics generally, the entanglement of denotation and connotation are mediated by the audience's fluent understanding learned through their encyclopedic competence and past experiences with similar works. In assessing these designs, the element of audience expectation and experience cannot be ignored. The transfers between static compositions—whether in paintings or children's books—and the particular motion composites of photography and typography employed in title designs unifies the semiotic organization of these forms, making the relations of reading::seeing a common foundation for them all.

Notes

1 Picarelli, E. "Aspirational Paratexts: The Case of 'Quality Openers' in TV Promotion." *Frames Cinema Journal*, 2013, http://framescinemajournal.com/article/aspirational-paratexts-the-case-of-quality-openers-in-tv-promotion-2/ accessed September 14, 2016.
2 Stanitzek, G. "Texts and Paratexts in Media." *Critical Inquiry*, Vol. 32, Autumn 2005, pp. 27–42.
3 Rand, P. *Thoughts on Design* (New York: Van Norstrand, 1970), p. 14.
4 Lupton, E. and A. Miller. *Design Writing Research: Writing on Graphic Design* (New York: Phaidon, 1996), p. 14.
5 Stanitzek, G. "Texts and Paratexts in Media." *Critical Inquiry*, Vol. 32, Autumn 2005, pp. 27–42.
6 Horak, J. *Saul Bass: Anatomy of Film Design* (Lexington: University of Kentucky Press, 2014).
7 Zagala, A. "The Edges of Film." *Senses of Cinema*, May 2002, Issue 20, http://sensesofcinema.com/2002/feature-articles/titles/ accessed September 14, 2016.
8 Landau, Solange. "Das Intro als eigenständige Erzählform. Eine Typologie." *Journal of Serial Narration on Television*, Vol. 1, no. 1, Spring 2013.
9 Eco, U. *A Theory of Semiotics* (Bloomington: Indiana University Press, 1979), pp. 137–138.
10 Barthes, R. *The Responsibility of Forms* (Berkeley: The University of California Press, 1985), p. 141.
11 Barthes, R. *The Responsibility of Forms* (Berkeley: The University of California Press, 1985), p. 137.
12 Ades, D. *Dalí's Optical Illusions* (New Haven: Yale University Press, 2000), p. 12.
13 Barthes, R. *The Responsibility of Forms* (Berkeley: The University of California Press, 1985), p. 131.
14 For example, see the online review, "The House on Skull Mountain (1974)." February 4, 2010, http://campblood.org/Newblog/archives/1777 accessed April 2, 2013.
15 Foucault, M. *The Birth of the Clinic* (New York: Vintage, 1975), p. xiii.
16 Barthes, R. *The Responsibility of Forms* (Berkeley: The University of California Press, 1985), p. 144.
17 Haskin, P. "Saul, Can You Make Me a Title?" *Film Quarterly*, Vol. 50, no. 1, Autumn 1996.
18 Golden, W. "Type Is to Read" in *The Visual Craft of William Golden*, ed. Cipe Pineles Golden, Kurt Weihs, and Robert Stunsky (New York: George Braziller, 1962), pp. 13–35.
19 Bass, S. "Some Thoughts on Motion Picture Film" in *Design Forecast 2*, ed. Samuel L. Fahnestock (Pittsburg: Alcoa, 1960), pp. 20–21.
20 Rosen, B. "The Man with the Golden Arm" in *The Corporate Search for Visual Identity* (New York: Van Norstrand, 1970), pp. 101–106.
21 Haskin, P. "Saul, Can You Make Me a Title?" *Film Quarterly*, Vol. 50, no. 1, Autumn 1996, pp. 12–13.

22 Rosen, B. “The Man with the Golden Arm” in *The Corporate Search for Visual Identity* (New York: Van Norstrand, 1970).
23 Stanitzek, G. “Reading the Title Sequence (*Vorspann, Génèrique*).” *Cinema Journal*, Vol. 48, no. 4, 2009, p. 45.
24 Stanitzek, G. “Reading the Title Sequence (*Vorspann, Génèrique*).” *Cinema Journal*, Vol. 48, no. 4, 2009, pp. 44–46.
25 Barthes, R. *Camera Lucida*, trans. Richard Howard (New York: Hill and Wang, 1981), p. 85.
26 Bazin, A. *What Is Cinema?*, trans. Timothy Barnard (Montreal: Caboose, 2009), pp. 8–9.
27 Markstein, D. “Walter Lantz.” *Don Markstein's Toonopedia*, http://www.toonopedia.com/lantz.htm accessed July 3, 2016.
28 Dunn, L. “Special Effects Cinematography.” *Journal of the University Film Association*, Vol. 26, no. 4, 1974, pp. 65–66.
29 Fielding, R. *The Technique of Special Effects Cinematography* (Oxford: Focal Press, 1984), pp. 405–406.

2

Type superimposed or composited over imagery is a commonplace part of graphic design and motion graphics. Other than simply filming a piece of reflective design, the placement of typography over a background image as an approach to combine type and image—whether animated or not, live action photography, or simply a static background—dominates the history of title sequences in film, television, and video games. The graphic organization of the screen, however, is not as monotonous as this singularity of technique might imply. How the audience understands the relationship between (foreground) typography and (background) image sets in motion a sequence of other, more grammatical dynamics of *reading::seeing* that produce the different interpretative modes. These semiotics of text–image combinations are determined by these lower-level identifications.

Audience perception of the relationship between typography and image determines their meaning: whether the typography and photography are recognized as being illustratively linked, or remain as separate, distinct "fields" on-screen is the fundamental judgment that organizes semiosis. The motion picture photography (employed as a background) and superimposed typography (title cards) emerge as two distinct elements readily distinguished from each other by the formal design of each title card. The most basic recognition of these compositions either invokes the direct relationship of a textual label attached to an identifying image (calligram), or asserts the independence of elements that lack an immediate connection (figure–ground). The 'discovery' of the relationship described by the rebus mode depends on higher-level recognitions separate from what is immediately apparent. All these modes originate with non-motion imagery familiar from children's books and play, but are most commonly encountered in motion pictures today. The distinction between linked and separate text–image composites is a transfer of this established experience learned with childhood picture books that is used to interpret similar design structures encountered later in life: as Michel Foucault has noted in his analysis of calligrams, these modes are paralinguistic semiotic structures acquired simultaneously with language fluency.

These modes originate with the same production technique—text superimposed/composited over a photograph, either in the fabrication of an answer print, or through optical printing. The figure–ground and calligram modes are immediate interpretations that organize how the audience watching a title sequence understands the individual title cards. Two title sequences used for feature films produced at Paramount Pictures in the mid-1930s demonstrate the common design of these modes' organization of text and image: Figure 2.1, from *Rumba* (Paramount, 1935), shows the *figure–ground mode* where the credits appear superimposed over shadows that have no immediately apparent, direct relationship to that text; Figure 2.2, from *The Big Broadcast of 1937* (Paramount, 1936), presents the *calligram mode*, discussed in Chapter 3. Each example presents a mutually exclusive interpretation of those elements contained by a specific title card (image, text), even though both title sequences employ both figure–ground and calligram modes. The higher-level *rebus mode* depends on complications of and modifications to the lower-level semiosis produced by this immediate recognition.

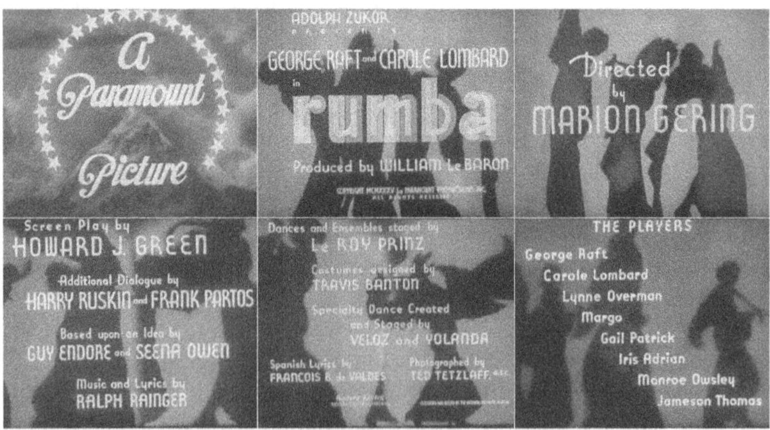

Figure 2.1 Title cards showing the figure–ground mode in *Rumba* (Paramount, 1935)

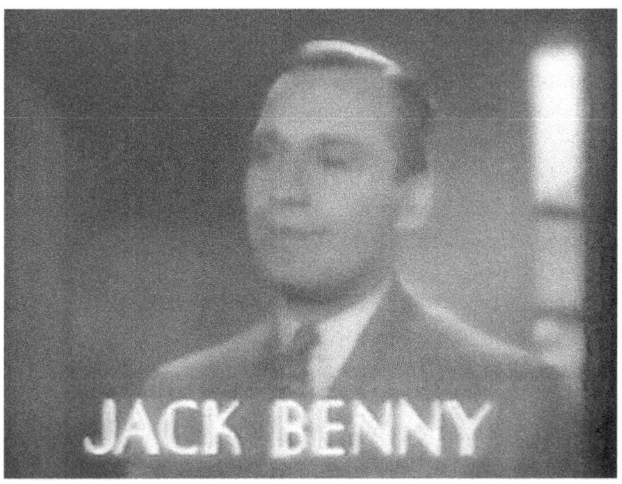

Figure 2.2 A calligram stating "Jack Benny" from *The Big Broadcast of 1937* (Paramount, 1936)

The Figure–Ground Mode

In this most basic mode, one reads the text (figure) and sees the image (ground) in a singular title card as entirely independent, unrelated elements. The figure–ground mode depends on this distinction between text and image. Reading and seeing are separated, and their interpretations remain uncorrelated. The figure–ground mode is foundational, apparent from the formal appearance of the individual title card itself. This mode has been common in title sequences throughout their history. The figure–ground mode [Figure 2.1] is historically the most common organization of image and text in title sequences: the text occupies one 'field' within the frame, and the other imagery falls into the 'background' (hence the designation of this mode as "figure–ground"). The separation between text and image is immediately apparent: one is *not* an illustration of the other, they are two separate, independent parts of the design that happen to appear on-screen together. The lack of direct correlation means that the development and meaning of the imagery (background) progresses without concern for what the text might state. The traditional visual structures of montage play out in the figure–ground mode modified only by how much the *disruption* potentially created by the text obscures the images: the title design by Byron Rabbitt for *Bad*

Girls Go to Hell (1965) demonstrates this *disruptive* effect that typography has for the background imagery.

Figure 2.1 has an allusive relationship between the background image and the superimposed text—the shadow-women are dressed in Spanish-looking clothes, and move around the screen in a way that suggests dance; the film is titled "Rumba." This linkage is to the film title itself, but is not a connection reflected in that specific title card since the 'dancing' begins in the middle of this six-card sequence, allowing the text and image in these title cards to remain conceptually distinct from each other. The ambiguity of this connection is typical for designs of this type. The background image does have a tangential relationship with the film title, as in both *Rumba* and *Bad Girls Go to Hell*—women in Spanish costumes dance behind the titles for *Rumba* (the connection of shadows and title may not even occur to a viewer), while the title montage in *Bad Girls Go to Hell* reveals what makes a "bad" girl.

This historically most common mode, where text and image are independent of one another, has many variations in design, yet the semiotic process remains constant: the texts (titles) and the imagery are simultaneously present on-screen, but are not linked as mutually illustrative demonstrations of the same thing. *Unknown* (2011) presents a variety of shots and is organized in an entirely different fashion than the 1935 title sequence, which is distinct and clearly separate from the narrative; in *Unknown*, the title sequence "as such" is effectively invisible, integrated with/into the beginning scenes of the dramatic narrative. Type placements in *Unknown* are integrated fully into the opening scenes of the motion picture itself, enabling the narrative to begin almost immediately. The text appears superimposed in unobtrusive ways that do not obscure the important actions on-screen, a tactic commonly employed in designs superimposed over opening narrative sequences since its introduction by Wayne Fitzgerald in 1958 for *Touch of Evil*. In designs produced prior to Fitzgerald's careful mapping of text into empty spaces on-screen, what magazine designers call "type hole"—voids in the composition of illustrations designed to contain text. The superimposed text in earlier designs disrupts the live action background material by covering it, as in *White Zombie* (1931) or *D.O.A.* (1949), whose title sequences run over the opening scenes of the narrative without consideration for these "background" images: these designs placed their text in the center of the screen, often fully obscuring the opening shots. In the case of *White Zombie*, the funeral at the crossroads that introduces voodoo to the audience is so completely hidden that the dialogue which follows the titles explicitly has to explain what was happening because for most of the long take the text fully obstructed the actions shown. What makes *Touch of Evil* important is Fitzgerald's novel solution to this disruptive effect—the title cards are composed *around* the live action, often placed near the margins of the shots so they do not obstruct the background narrative at all. This solution allows the narrative to run continuously, as in *Unknown*, eliding the independence of the title sequence from the rest of the film. Nevertheless, the formal relationship of superimposed title cards to background images specific to the figure–ground mode remains unchanged. The audience watching these titles does not identify a linkage between the background images and the texts superimposed over them.

Superimposed text and background image are in their own, independent fields of comprehension: there is no intersection of meaning or generation of new meaning in their combination because image and text are conceptually discrete. This distinction remains constant across the historical development of titles. The figure–ground mode employs clear demarcations between reading and seeing—the text and image remain distinct, independent of each other: they are separate, independent "fields" that have no immediately apparent relationship, nor do they imply a connection. Historically, it is common for the text superimposed over a background during the title sequence to entirely obscure this foundational photography. In this regard there is no significant interpretive difference between a title card employing the figure–ground mode made in 1935 from one made almost seventy-five years later in 2011. In both cases, these title cards present text that is unrelated to its background imagery, affirming the different natures of text and image.

The interpretive tension of reading::seeing is resolved in favor of the linguistic. By being designated "background," the photography becomes simply a visual accompaniment, a "decoration" that enlivens the design when it is separate from the live action as in *Rumba*. But these relations are inverted in *Unknown*. Instead of being an insignificant background provided as incidental to the text, because the title sequence is integrated with the opening scenes of the film, the typography is secondary to the activities dramatized on-screen. In *Unknown*, ignoring the text and focusing on the "background" image is not only appropriate, it is expected—the drama and its unfolding on-screen render the title cards secondary. The text becomes a *non-signifying* element for the opening narrative; the sense that the titles have been elided from this film is acute since their presence on-screen has no role in the drama that has started. Remaining in their own fields, the text and image enter into (almost) no significant relationships (there are a few calligrams in this design, presented *en passant*).

Title Montages

'Montage' is a well theorized topic in film studies. Having been initially proposed by the Soviet film makers in the 1920s, it has remained a focus of historical and critical examination in the decades since; however, in title sequences, it renders the dynamics of type and image as secondary—the relationship of text and image tends to be insignificant, leaving the more familiar structures of images joined and juxtaposed over time to produce meaning separate from the images' relationship to the typography—typical of the figure–ground mode. This use of montage is fundamentally independent of the text, a demonstration of how these elements remain distinct in the figure–ground mode.

The title sequence montage for *Bad Girls Go to Hell* (1965) demonstrates how the disruptive effects of superimposed typography function in relation to the background imagery, while still providing a necessary informational preamble about what makes a "bad" girl particular to the sexploitation genre. The montage resembles the rest of the film narrative that takes place in monotonous apartments that all look interchangeable, exactly the type of interior appearing in this opening montage: each setting provides an 'excuse' for the heroine to disrobe and lounge on the sofa, the bed, or in the kitchen—the nudity on-screen being the film's principal attraction (the definition of all sexploitation films, both the early 1960s 'nudie-cutie' as well as the later 1960s 'roughie' that *Bad Girls Go to Hell* invented).[1] While nudity was entirely forbidden in commercial cinema distributed by the Hollywood studios, an explicit invocation of voyeurism in a title sequence was still possible, but rare prior to the end of the Hollywood Production Code in 1968. There are few parallels to the *Bad Girls Go to Hell* title sequence from Hollywood studio productions: the titles for *Flamingo Road* (1949) is one of the few examples, other than those titles created for the James Bond films by Robert Brownjohn (*From Russia With Love*, 1963; *Goldfinger*, 1964) and Maurice Binder (*Thunderball*, 1965).

The 2-minute title design for this film was made at B & O Film Effects, the optical house credited in these titles (see title card no. 5 in Figure 2.3); no particular designer is specifically identified. A similar approach to the title design appears in Wishman's next film, *Indecent Desires* (1967), made under her pseudonym "Louis Sullivan." While these two title sequences are very similar, the voyeuristic element that appears in the second half of *Bad Girls Go to Hell* runs throughout *Indecent Desires*. Its titles were produced by the New York-based documentary and instructional film company B & O Film Specialists, Inc.; these two post-production companies (B & O Film Effects and B & O Film Specialists, Inc.) are in fact the same company. Although the title designs are uncredited on Wishman's films (an absence that is not surprising given the socially marginal character of sexploitation films), both designs were probably created by animator Byron Rabbit, who was on staff at B & O Film Specialists as their title designer. He did receive on-screen credit for the popular 1964 TV documentary series *Decision: The*

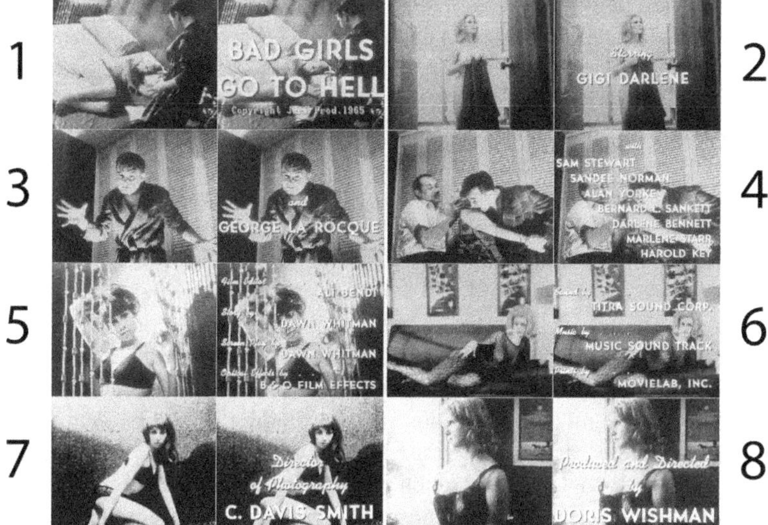

Figure 2.3 Title cards showing the montage from *Bad Girls Go to Hell* (1965)

Trials of Harry S. Truman, a socially responsible series of twenty-six half-hour episodes made by Screen Gems in which the former President reflected on his career.[2] The relative unreliability of *all* the credits in both *Bad Girls Go to Hell* and *Indecent Desires* is a reflection of how common pseudonyms are throughout the sexploitation genre, a dimension of these productions that continues in later pornographic films. As film critic Christopher J. Jarmick noted in his profile of director Doris Wishman's career for *Senses of Cinema* in 2002, Wishman was one of the few woman producer/directors to work on low-budget sexploitation films in the 1960s. She produced and directed under several pseudonyms as well as using her own name, making a total of thirty films, with the majority—twenty-six—between 1959 and 1977. Her first film, *Hide Out in the Sun* (1959), was a pioneering exploitation film of the post-World War II period that would influence later sexploitation directors such as Dave Friedman and Hershel Gordon Lewis.[3] *Bad Girls Go to Hell* (1965) was described as a "cult classic" by the New York Times in her 2002 obituary.[4]

Rabbit's designs in both films are consistent, resulting in a steady progression through these 2-minute long sequences. Every 'title card' is composed from two distinct elements: a full-frame still image, and then the same image with text optically printed over it. The pairing of still image followed by text superimposition gives these title sequences a rhythmic character—all the cards are uniform in length and timing as the superimposed type fades up on each image, giving them a presentational character: the audience sees each still picture clearly before it is partially obscured behind the text. It is a design approach that enables an identification of the image content independently of the text. This approach reiterates the figure::ground relationship with each new card, separating the text and image fully and allowing the familiar functions of montage to dominate the sequence even as the text receives both equal screen time and equal weight graphically in the construction of this opening sequence.

There are eight title card/still image pairs in *Bad Girls Go to Hell* [Figure 2.3]; five of these title cards (numbers 2, 5, 6, 7, and 8) invoke the typical viewer relationship common to pin-ups and other voyeuristic photographs: they present what appears to be two (or possibly three) different female models in various states of undress. The first half of the sequence, title cards 1–4, suggests a narrative montage; the second half, title cards 5–8, contains production credits, but unlike the earlier implied narrative, each image is clearly posed and resembles conventional pin-up imagery. Title cards 6, 7, and 8 invoke voyeurism via the conventional 'direct address' these women have of their (unseen) audience—they gaze calmly and directly into the camera.

These title designs develop a consistent voyeuristic theme of women being watched—either by a man shown in the title card, or implicitly via direct address to the audience, or through her apparent engagement with someone unseen, but present off-screen. These relationships between display and being-watched run throughout the entire montage in *Bad Girls Go to Hell*. This presentation of nudity is one of the 'attractions' offered by the film itself: it is a variation on the 'nudie-cutie,' inaugurating a new subgenre, the 'roughie.' The design of this title sequence around both an implied narrative of voyeurism and violence, as well as the more conventionally recognizable pin-up, is an acknowledgment of the formal nature of sexploitation films produced during the 1960s—their primary box-office draw was the presentation of on-screen female nudity: two of the pin-up images, title cards 2 and 8, both show the same woman in a bathroom scene that implies a spied-upon encounter between that woman and another, unseen party—yet, unlike the other pin-up styled photographs, this woman does not appear aware of the camera and her gaze does not address the viewer. This spied-upon aspect is part of the implied narrative of the first four title cards. Of the remaining three title cards (numbers 1, 3, and 4), all show the same woman as in title cards 2 and 8. While all the title cards also have a voyeuristic character, this smaller group is distinguished from the others by their implied immanent violence and trauma: two suggest moments immediately prior to a (sexual) assault (title cards 1 and 3), while the third (title card 4) shows what appears to be the assault itself. Coupled with the superimposed text in title card 1, "Bad Girls Go to Hell," the violence of these images—and the more traditional pin-ups of the other title cards—reconfigures this entire sequence not as an exercise *in* voyeurism, but as moralizing *about* voyeurism even as it employs it: the 'Hell' suggested within this title sequence is one where the (very real) fourth wall of photography/cinema collapses and the female models within these images become subject to what might otherwise be *imaginary* acts by their audience. The immanent eruption of sex/violence within this title is linked to both the nature of the film, sexploitation ('roughie'), and to the title itself, "Bad Girls Go to Hell."

The title sequence raises and implies the answer to what makes a "bad girl" as well as what constitutes "hell"—in both cases the answer is the same: *sex*. The voyeuristic elements of this design and the transition to the violent 'roughie' that *Bad Girls Go to Hell* defined make this connection of sex to hell explicit. The narrative emerges *because* of female sexualization; the plot chronicles the aftermath of the heroine, "Meg Kelton" (played by Gigi Darlene, whose title card is a calligram), killing her would-be rapist. The film's narrative follows her without cutting away to chronicle the other characters she encounters; she is the central (and only) focus of the film. Film theorist Laura Mulvey's characterization of the female "exhibitionist role," in her essay "Visual Pleasure and Narrative Cinema" written in 1975, while *not* directly concerned with the sexploitation genre, effectively describes the problem posed by this film made by a female director for a specifically male audience. That her theory's critical understanding of voyeurism puts the female viewers of such films in a distinctly *masochistic* position is a fact acknowledged by title card 3, where the audience is momentarily positioned as the woman who is assaulted—an identification in this singular image that is challenged by the other images of this title sequence. This disavowal and simultaneous embrace of these tendencies becomes an issue for Wishman's later productions in the 1970s—she would pass the direction of the explicit scenes of her pornographic films to her male production crew, literally leaving the set for those scenes.[5]

Film theorist Laura Mulvey's analysis of voyeuristic relations precisely explains the formal organization of the title sequence for *Bad Girls Go to Hell*, as well as the film's individual scenes, which are constructed in an idiosyncratic fashion in which static shots of objects in the rooms interrupt the actions on-screen, appearing as tangents that disrupt the action, deflecting attention away from "Meg Kelton"—*her body*—and what happens to her. Yet at the same time, these peculiar cut-aways function to make the voyeuristic gaze that much more apparent.[6] The intrusive voyeurism that starts in the title sequence is representative of the film as a whole:

> In their traditional exhibitionist role women are simultaneously looked at and displayed, with their appearance coded for strong visual and erotic impact so they can be said to connote *to-be-looked-at-ness*. Women displayed as a sexual object is the leit-motif of erotic spectacle: from pin-ups to strip-tease, from Ziegfeld to Busy Berkeley, she holds the look, plays to and signifies male desire.[7]

Mulvey's recognition of the *on-displayness* characteristic of eroticized imagery is evident throughout the scenario itself, where each scene serves as a new opportunity to see the heroine shed her clothes. However, in spite of its freely displayed female body, the sexuality on display is not a 'free' one (in the sense of 1960s "free love")—it is a trap, a prison, contained—this linkage may seem surprising given the generic affinities of *Bad Girls Go to Hell*. The transition from 'nudie-cutie' into the more violent 'roughie' brings the masochistic dimensions of this production into relief: written and directed by a woman, it is focused on continuously threatening "Meg Kelton" (the heroine) with punishment for killing her assailant in self-defense. This dimension of impending violence is overlaid onto a title sequence that is evenly divided between posed, conventional pin-up imagery and narrative imagery; title cards 3 and 4 have an explicit violent content and card 1 suggests violence as a man stands over a naked woman lying in a bed. This impression is developed in/by card 3, a calligram stating 'George La Rocque' (pseudonym of Charles E. Mazin), who appears with arms spread open leaning forward in a threateningly direct way; in card 4 he is joined by a second man, assaulting her in a suggestively sexual way that is nevertheless explicitly violent—both sex and violence are linked in this entire opening sequence, answering what a "bad girl" is—*one who is sexually available*—and implying what constitutes "hell"—the male attention such girls receive. This suggestion of what makes a 'bad girl' implicitly arises from the film's title is contained by its title sequence—implied in the formal quotations (pin-ups) that inform each still image—that sex leads to violence, that sex is violent—gives the development of the titles and the entire film a moralizing tone that runs counter to its production and marketing (sexploitation film), challenging the voyeuristic dimensions of the sexual spectacle that is the primary focus of both titles and narrative. This recognition of what is "bad" is a function of the montage in relation to the film's title rather than through a juxtaposition in relation to any particular title card. The separate fields of "figure" and "ground" are maintained throughout this sequence.

Those title cards that follow this opening scene of primal violence assume an almost fetishistic quality in their disavowal of both nudity and the violence that accompanies it: in the first two title cards, female nudity is emphatically on view, even when it has been mitigated, in each case, by either her pose (seen from behind) or by holding a prop (the towel she holds in front of her body); in title card 4, she is dressed in the same transparent garment worn in both cards 6 and 8. Yet even when 'dressed,' the impact of these stills is of nudity—the conventional nature of the pin-up is to be 'dressed' in such a way that the 'clothes' perform a seduction, implying their *immanent* removal if not their *insubstantiality* (via transparent fabrics and/or lace). This is a title sequence (as well as a film) that could never meet the demands imposed by the Hollywood Production Code's moral restrictions on depiction that literally begins with a refusal of any suggestion of nudity:

(1) The more intimate parts of the human body are male and female organs and the breasts of a *woman.*

   (a) They should never be uncovered.
   (b) They should not be covered with transparent or translucent material.
   (c) They should not be clearly and unmistakably outlined by the garment.[8]

Obviously, both the narrative content of the film and the still photographic backgrounds to the titles would be immediately censored by this restriction on any *suggestion* of nudity; the actual nudity readily apparent in the titles (and appearing throughout the film) was forbidden *a priori* by the Production Code. The sexploitation genre was defined by precisely this difference with the Hollywood studio productions—the depiction of what was repressed[9] in studio production is these film's commercial 'attraction.' The precise restrictions imposed by this code are all directly flaunted by title cards 4, 5, 6, 7, and 8, all of which present situations that directly violate 1b and 1c of the code, quoted above. In designing a title sequence constructed around such immediately apparent violations of this code, these titles announce a transgressive quality that is both challenged by and reinforced through the apparent violence and voyeurism of the sequence as a whole.

The conventional representations employed by the lurid dust jackets and book covers of "sleaze paperbacks" informs the style of imagery used throughout *Bad Girls Go to Hell*; this subgenre of publishing exaggerates the (restrained) voyeurism of the romance novel cover into imagery that borrows the form of the pin-up. The reiteration of these tropes in the design for *Bad Girls Go to Hell* is what makes this design both critical and complicit with its voyeurism: while the viewer relationship with the imagery reaffirms the typical (male) spectatorial position that Mulvey describes, it is also one where the audience is put in the position of the woman-being-assaulted, if only momentarily, in title card 3: 'George La Rocque' stands in a confrontational posture, advancing in a gesture of direct address. The only narrative 'position' that makes sense for this particular shot is that of the *woman's* point-of-view. By momentarily positioning the audience as the subject of the assault, rather than in the position of the man doing that assault, it challenges the more traditional framings of the other shots in the sequence. Title cards 1 and 4 have a difference valence in context with title card 3, even though they do *not* escape from the traditional modeling of woman-to-be-looked-at, an awareness of what the man-who-looks entails undercuts these shots with a subversive awareness that when woman looks back we do not see her gaze, a fact made emphatically clear in title card 2.

The intractability of the traditional depictive relationship of the on-screen woman's to-be-looked-at-ness, modeled for (both) male characters on-screen and male audience, contains the critical aspects of this title sequence before their critical dimensions develop: the challenge posed by the first half of the sequence is effectively disavowed by the second half's replacement of narrative with pin-up imagery. While the entire sequence alludes to the designs of "sleaze paperbacks," it is the insistent reassertion of standard voyeuristic structures and imagery that forestalls the critique from progressing. Instead, the dynamic of voyeurism—disavowal—violence structures not only the title sequence but the narrative itself: the seemingly random insert shots of objects within the rooms where the action of the film plays out act as disavowals of the voyeurism even as it continues, transitioning to violence, as Mulvey notes in her analysis:

> The male unconscious has two avenues of escape: preoccupation with the re-enactment of the original trauma (investigating the woman, demystifying her mystery), counterbalanced by devaluation, punishment or saving of the guilty object (an avenue typified by the concerns of film noir); or else complete disavowal of castration by the substitution of a fetish object or turning the repressed figure itself into a fetish so that it becomes reassuring rather than dangerous (hence overvaluation, the cult of the female star).[10]

What is striking about the insert shots (identified as a feature of Wishman's style common to all her sexploitation films) is that their function in the film is not as a substitution or fetish, but as an interruption of the voyeuristic imagery itself. The same stoppage that appears during the narrative action is created by the recurring fragmentation of the montage's progression—a progression that stops for each superimposed text—each 'stoppage' complicates the connections of one shot to the next. These texts force the audience to consider each image as a semi-isolated still; the reversion to voyeuristic structures contained by the narrative sequences demands a violent repudiation. These momentary interruptions that define the structure of the titles themselves—reveal that it is no accident that the violence of the first title cards is directly followed by what Mulvey would identify as 'fetish' imagery ('pin-ups') where the female subjects directly address the (unseen) viewer in a display of sensuous (optical) availability essential to the 'pin-up' as a particular visual form. The violence that is accentuated by the text-interruptions is thus banished by the shift in background imagery.

The organization of both titles and narrative in *Bad Girls Go to Hell* is homologous: the critical dimensions of this production are at one and the same time countered by its complicity with its own voyeuristic spectacle. The relationship it has to traditional depictions of women on display for an (assumed) male audience—the pin-up, the "sleaze paperback," Hollywood's "glamor shot" are the fundamental condition of both the title sequence and the film narrative, their *raison d'être*—is simultaneously structured in the film *as* trauma: *Bad Girls Go to Hell* conceives of "hell" as simultaneously female sexuality *and* the attraction it has over men (and other women), causing the devaluation, punishment, and violence that defines this film as a 'roughie.' The collapse of the initial critical dimensions of the title sequence montage into conventional pin-up photography is repeated by the insert shots that interrupt the narrative drama itself. These breaks in the continuous flow suggest the same anxiety emergent in this opening montage where active female sexuality becomes punishment—the 'hell' of dislocation, abandonment, and loss of family and friends the heroine experiences over the course of the film, a structural logic that develops and proceeds entirely apart from the punctuating texts that interrupt the montage's progression. The title montage encapsulates and symbolizes events *elsewhere* in the motion picture, yet what distinguishes the montage in a title sequence from the narrative drama itself is precisely the continuous return to text that interrupts this development. The background images are is a distinct representation denoting meaning *for* and *about* the remainder of the program. The montage thus functions as a sign whose reference is the narrative, as semiotician Umberto Eco explains:

> Signs are natural events that act as symptoms or indices, and they entertain with that which they designate a relation based in the mechanism of inference (if such a symptom, then such a sickness; if smoke, then fire).[11]

The meaning of the title montage is denotative; the sequence as a whole is organized as a sign for the production that follows. This understanding of the title sequence is the "traditional view" that the opening should encapsulate the meaning of the narrative. The use of montage in *Bad Girls Go to Hell* follows this formal prescription. The meaning of the title montage illuminates events in the remainder of the program—the actual drama that is the represented meaning enables the substitution of interpretations within a constrained framework, as Peter Wollen notes in his discussion of Charles Saunders Peirce's conception of semiotics in relation to motion pictures in his book *Signs and Meaning in the Cinema*:

> An icon, according to Pierce, is a sign which resembles its object mainly by its similarity to it. . . . An index is a sign by virtue of an existential bond between itself and its object. . . . The third category of signs, the symbol, corresponds to Saussure's arbitrary sign. Like Saussure, Pierce speaks of a contract by virtue of which the symbol is a sign.
>
> Unlike verbal language, the cinema is, as we have seen, primarily indexical and iconic. It is the symbolic which is the submerged dimension.[12]

Pierce's theory provides two categories for interpretations based upon denotation: the icon and the index. The 'index' identifies not the meaning but the factors that enable a particular conclusion—the image itself in the title montage provides this element—the resemblance of the thing for itself (a chair represents a chair, and so on), and those conclusions we draw based on the observable characteristics of that form—while the symbolic standing-for that we normally encounter in language is often absent. However, this relationship becomes uncertain in the title montage for *Bad Girls Go to Hell* because it is understood as metonymously related to, perhaps even excerpts from, the (future) events in the drama. This recognition shifts these images' meaning to reveal crucial yet partial information. Isolated from the drama, they function as exemplars. What matters is not the resemblance between the events portrayed on-screen, but the resemblance between 'this shot' and the other shots yet-to-be-seen within the narrative that follows the montage: the standard intertextual relationship of title sequence to drama.

Television Opener Montages

'Montage' as symbolic ordering is innate to the history of this practice in motion pictures, yet the typical organization of these sequences does not subordinate them to the liminal demands focused around title designs. The index that makes the title sequence's structures coherent is only partly the specifics of its imagery—to function as an introduction to a larger work, much like the book covers, blurbs, and other paratexts that Gérard Genette discusses in *Paratexts: Thresholds of Interpretation* as the interface between the interiority of narrative and exteriority of life.[13] To function as an introduction demands that the title montage's meaning be linked to the narrative that follows. Rama Allen's title sequence for the historical drama *Vikings* (2013), a dramatic television program focused on the Viking's invention of 'long boats' capable of reaching England (and based on Viking myths about Ragnar Lodbrok[14]). The series details the impact this invention has on their society.

German media historian Solange Landau's research into the design and structure of television openings has termed this type of television title sequence the "Ästhetische Intro" (Aesthetic Intro), in which the title sequence is an independent unit that presents an "interpretation" of the series' themes and may not contain any actors or make direct reference to what appears in the show.[15] As is typical for the "Ästhetische Intro," the narrative drama only plays an indirect role in the organization of the title sequence itself. Produced in collaboration with Art Director Audrey Davis at The Mill, *Vikings* employs a montage built around a lone figure, who does not appear in the program, sinking into murky, dark water as emblematic objects sink past him: coins, a helmet, an axe. Following the premiere of the show in 2013, it was been recognized by the motion graphics industry as an exceptional design, and has been profiled in several of the field's industry publications.[16]

Revisited and updated in 2015, both the original and the update are unusual: neither title sequence presents the show's cast. There are no cameos, cut scenes, or any of the typical presentations of each character in vignette during this opening sequence. Instead, the design is a prime example of figure–ground mode operative throughout the entire montage. The imagery is evocative of its historical setting without presenting particular stories or events from the show itself, resulting in an apparently self-contained title sequence that is the definitional feature of Landau's "Ästhetische Intro." This opening runs 52 seconds and presents a distinct visual style that differs stylistically from the primary narrative: Allen's title sequence uses highly expressionistic lighting, framing of shots, and sequencing of edits. In contrast, the program portrays the reign of terror that accompanied Viking raids on the lands to their south with highly detailed realism. Organized rhythmically around the song "If I Had a Heart" (2009) by the Swedish band Fever Ray, the images are cut to the music in an irregular fashion—flash frames that contrast with the dark water are cut against the drowning man's descent, clearly distinguished from the blues and blacks that otherwise fill the sequence. These shots imply glimpsed memories, the "life flashing before one's eyes" at the moment of death, as noted by Allen in an interview with *Forget the Film, Watch the Titles* about his design: "At the heart, this title sequence is about the space between life and death, and one person crossing that gap."[17] However, his narrative-based interpretation does not preclude other, more metaphoric interpretations of these titles. These cut-ins are on-screen just long enough to suggest their violent content, and it is this violence that dominates this opening title sequence whose overall movement is downwards: everything that moves, travels down the screen. It is a subtle effect that amplifies the hallucinatory character of this descent into darkness, suggesting that the dominant image of this title sequence—the drowning man—is essentially metaphoric, that the 'drowning' is more than just a literal submersion in turbulent water, it is a submersion into and by violence.

The violence of this opening sequence is implied, rather than shown: it is a symbolically invoked violence. This metaphoric image is of the drowning man sinking into the depths is amplified by a series of brief, flash frames. It is possible to watch the sequence and not be consciously aware of their presence, yet they are significant for the affect of this title design and have a significant role in developing its metaphoric character. The insert flashes are a series of shots that look like nothing more than the storm clouds and lightning flashes that accompany an approaching storm, but on closer inspection several of these shots contain a grey, hooded figure [Figure 2.4] revealed by the lightning: initially at a great distance, then in (almost) medium shot. It is a terrifying image in its suggestion of a death-figure advancing an enormous distance in between the two lightning flashes—in the second shot it appears to have a skull for a face.

The second insert, unlike the first group of storm clouds and lightning that are almost indistinguishable, contrasts strongly with the rest of the proximate sequence: they are brightly lit and are dominated by brilliant areas of white where the rest of the sequence is nearly black; the first shot shows two bloody hands against an indistinct background of grass and white, overexposed sky. The second shot shows a woman's face in close-up, caressed by a bloody hand; the third shot shows an extreme close-up of a hand doing something (it is unclear what) with what appears to be meat.

This element of immanent threat becomes explicit 26 seconds into the sequence (the midpoint) with a series of graphic-match edits: waves crash onto black, jagged rocks; cut to swirling sparks and flames around a horse with bit and bridle coming into shot; cut to a black bird (a raven or crow) swooping in among the sparks to roost, shown in a pair of shots, its black eye flashing silver as it bends its head [Figure 2.5]. This short sequence of edits at the center of the title identifies the drowning man as submerged within a sea of violence: literally the violently crashing waves of this dark sea become a burst of flames, burning sparks swirling in place of the sea's

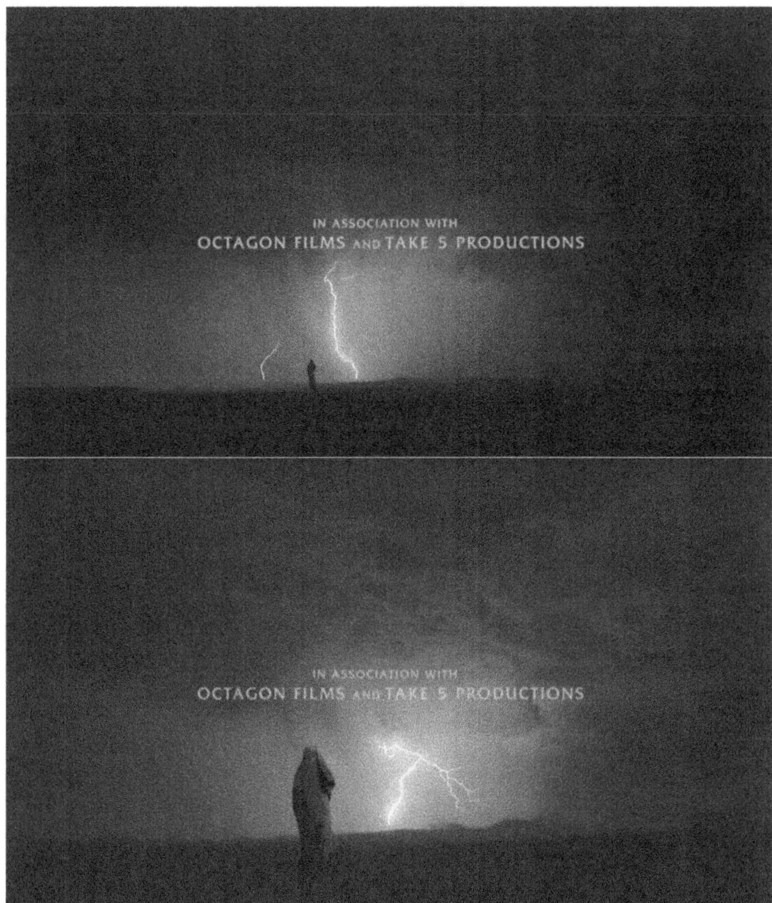

Figure 2.4 Title cards showing approaching figure from *Vikings* (season 1, 2013)

spray. Such a transformation dramatizes the metaphor of a 'tide of violence,' rendering it as a visceral reality on-screen.

Understanding this narrative about Viking raids in terms of their literal actions and metaphysical significance—rather than through a presentation of the actors with their roles as would be more typical of a television program's opening montage, what historian Landau's has termed "Mosaik-Intro" (Mosaic Intro) in which the title sequence introduces the lead actors and their characters showing them "in action" via short scenes extracted from the episodes that follow.[18] This expository activity unifies the imagery

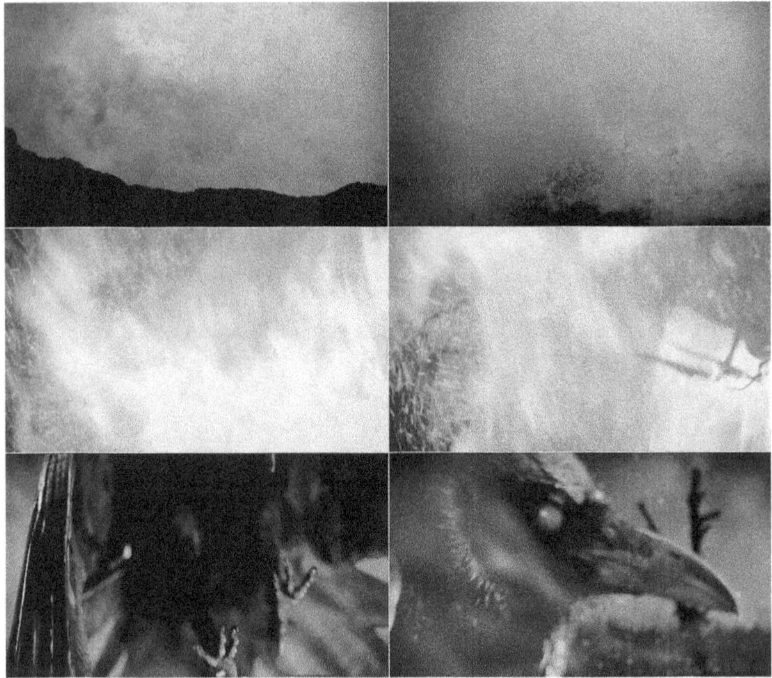

Figure 2.5 Stills showing graphic matches in the montage from *Vikings* (season 1, 2013)

via a montage that summarizes the premise while at the same time highlighting the actors. These sequences may not include title cards for these actors, instead developing towards a singular reveal of the program's title and dispersing actual credits as superimposed text over the start of the narrative after the program begins.

The titles [Figure 2.6] for the ABC-produced crime drama *Castle* (2009–2016) are typical of "Mosaic Intro" title montages produced by and aired on the broadcast television networks CBS, NBC, and ABC in the United States. Title montages are often seasonally revised—what the television industry calls the "refresh" (a common feature of the montages used by shows broadcast on ABC, CBS, and NBC)—so they always incorporate shots drawn from yet-to-be-seen stories. Variation is central to this periodic redesign; by incorporating new material from the new season's episodes, the audience encounters the updated title sequence aware that they are watching an ongoing series, with the anticipation that the title montage will be a combination

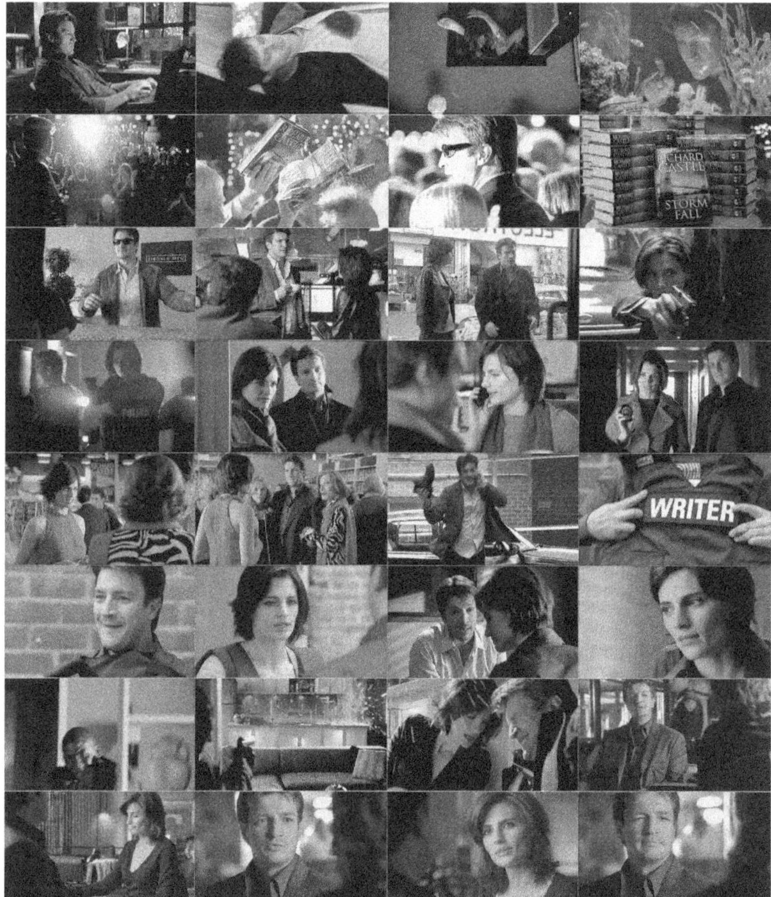

Figure 2.6 Stills showing the "Mosaic Intro" montage from *Castle* (season 2, 2010)

of what they have already seen with material they will see later. The montages in *Castle* are typical: they use the same live action shots that (re)appear in the program with no obvious changes, resulting in an ambivalent relationship to the program itself: it is this ambivalence about the scenes these shots imply—is the action shown part of the current episode about to be seen, a past episode already seen, or one not yet seen—that enables the title montage to function as non-diegetic narrative exposition where each "refresh" involves a transformation of the visual content in the montage. This fact remains constant in all "refreshed" title montages, whether they are for a program with an ongoing story that continues from episode to episode, or not. Once constructed, these "refreshed" montage sequences will typically remain unchanged for an entire "season" (typically twenty-two episodes).

The season 2, 3, and 4 title sequence "refreshes" for *Castle* (2010, 2011, 2012) expand the initial title-card-only opening of season 1 into a complex series of shots unified by music and voice-over into a coherent singular unit (the precise combination of shots changes slightly with each season's montage); there was no montage for the first season of episodes, even though the logo design will reappear at the end of the montage sequences used in later seasons. These titles explain the premise for the show: a mystery writer who accompanies a homicide detective in solving crimes in New York City. This montage is used without change throughout season 2, but not all of the shots in it are from season 1; some of them from (what are at the start of season 2) *future* episodes—these images are not ones the audience could have seen previously. It begins with a shot of a man sitting at a computer typing, followed by shots of the same man (Nathan Fillion, who plays "Rick Castle," the title character) wearing sun glasses while being photographed in a bookstore. Over these shots a male voice-over says, "There are two kinds of folks who sit around thinking about how to kill people: psychopaths and mystery writers. I'm the kind that pays better. Who am I?" This opening question is not rhetorical—it is answered in the diegetic sound for the shots where the same man who appears in the first shot says "Castle" several times in a row, identifying both the main character and the program title simultaneously, while responding affirmatively to the voice-over's question. There are no title cards in this opening montage, only an animated logo resolve at its conclusion. Because it so fully subordinates the individual cut scenes to the final reveal of the show title, making this animated title card a restatement of what has already been established earlier in the montage sequence, it answers the opening voice-over's question: *who am I?* This mixture of statement and reiteration is implicit in the choice of shots and how the final logo animation for *Castle* appears as a series of letters "lighting up" synchronized to plucked guitar strings, an animation introduced in season 1 and retained for the refreshed titles [Figure 2.7]. Each season's title montage for *Castle* maintains this organization of cut scenes, voice-over, and animated logo. The montage proceeds by explicitly quoting from the program's narrative events in a self-conscious fashion: this acknowledgment of the relationship with its source is evident to the audience for these title designs—its audience's past experience and deployment of that knowledge, while for new viewers, it provides a brief summary of the narrative's assumptions. The montage relays the program's "back story": who the central character "Rick Castle" is and what the premise of how the detective genre program *will* proceed. This expository activity unifies the imagery around a self-contained narrative that

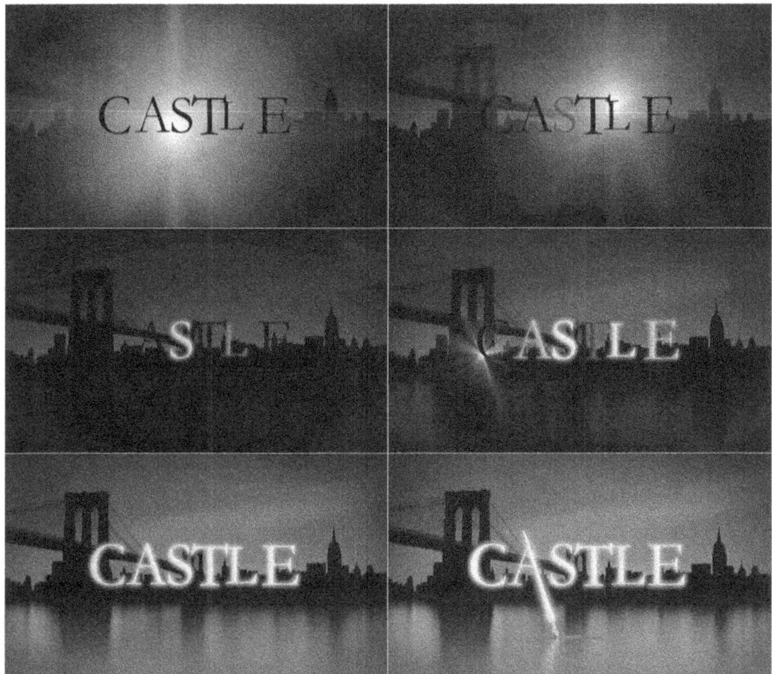

Figure 2.7 Title card animation from *Castle* (season 1, 2009)

summarizes the program premise. The montage sequence re-presents earlier shots and scenes from the first (and second) seasons, acting as a reminder and teaser about (future) events of the current episode/season.

Audiences recognize the title montage is quotational, even if they do not recognize the quotations in themselves; in making the montage, the identification of these individual shots as "cut scenes" means they are a variation on an established set of potentials. Cut scenes have a specifically intertextual relationship with the program they accompany. The result is neither entirely "repetitive" nor "quotational," but rather transformative, resulting in an entirely new meaning emerging from how each clip fits together to explain the character's interrelationships to each other and the 'background' to the narrative, in excess to a basic communication of the show's premise. When the scenes that are 'quoted' by the title montage do finally appear on-screen, what the audience recognizes is that the scene had already been shown in the title sequence—the relationship of source to quotation flows backwards, changing the program into the quotation of the titles. The confusion of relationships that emerges tacitly in this transformation is one in which the linkage of titles and program becomes more direct and immediate: it validates the claims of the title montage as a representation of the series—the preamble is an accurate portrayal of the program; the individual episodes then become simply variations on the premises established in the title sequence itself. The absurd implication that the particular episode is simply an elaboration of potentials contained by the title sequence is nevertheless implicit in this reversal of relationships between source and quotation, but is not something the audience necessarily considers while watching the titles themselves.

What matters is not the resemblance between the events portrayed on-screen, but the resemblance between 'this shot' and the other shots yet-to-be-seen within the narrative that follows the titles: an intertextual relationship of quotation to source material, not reality to source material. The subordination of the title montage to the narrative is thus doubled by the quotational montage, even more than in the "independent" sequence. The immediate referent—the program—de-emphasizes the iconic and indexical dimensions of the montage as a photographic (visual) document and focuses its organization around the linkages to the narrative-to-come. Whether it includes superimposed text or not is irrelevant to this lexical organizational of the images. Their selection is precisely based on their capacity to evoke some meaning in relation to the primary drama.

The figure–ground mode is the simplest relationship between superimposed text and image: the audience recognizes the independence of these two fields; while their composition together may be orchestrated to create an aesthetic arrangement, they are nevertheless fully independent of each other. In distinguishing between text and image, the dominance of the text as a primary focus—even in "artful" compositions—is determined by the need for it to be legible. The complexity or subtlety of the design thus reflects the arrangement of these separate domains. Text and image necessarily converge as the finished composite, but in the figure–ground mode, the combination is a technical fact that leaves the image and text as parallel articulations within a unified composition. Once they begin entering into mutual relations as juxtaposed and convergent elements producing meaning, the text–image composite becomes a different mode: either a calligram, or a rebus depending on the nature of their connection.

Notes

1 Martin, D. "Doris Wishman, 'B' Film Director, Dies." *The New York Times*, August 19, 2002.

2 "Decision: The Conflicts of Harry S. Truman." *The Harry S. Truman Library and Museum*, https://www.trumanlibrary.org/decision/videos.htm accessed September 16, 2016.

3 Jarmick, C. "Great Directors: Doris Wishman." *Senses of Cinema*, October 2002, Issue 22, http://sensesofcinema.com/2002/great-directors/wishman/ accessed April 1, 2014.
4 Martin, D. "Doris Wishman, 'B' Film Director, Dies." *The New York Times*, August 19, 2002.
5 Jarmick, C. "Great Directors: Doris Wishman." *Senses of Cinema*, October 2002, Issue 22, http://sensesofcinema.com/2002/great-directors/wishman/ accessed April 1, 2014. C. Davis Smith, her cinematographer on these films, stated: "One thing, though, Doris would not shoot the explicit scenes. She would say, 'Go ahead and do what you have to!' retiring to another room until we told her we were done shooting."
6 Jarmick notes that the idiosyncrasies of the cut-aways were used to avoid technical problems with sync sound; however, they also function as disruptions in the spectacle of female nudity on-screen. "Great Directors: Doris Wishman." *Senses of Cinema*, October 2002, Issue 22, http://sensesofcinema.com/2002/great-directors/wishman/ accessed April 1, 2014.
7 Mulvey, L. "Visual Pleasure and Narrative Cinema" in *Film Theory and Criticism: Introductory Readings*, ed. Leo Braudy and Marshall Cohen (New York: Oxford University Press, 1999), p. 837.
8 This version of the production code was reprinted in Dogherty, Thomas. *Pre-Code Hollywood: Sex, Immorality, and Insurrection in American Cinema; 1930–1934* (New York: Columbia University Press; 2nd edition, 1999).
9 Maltby, R. "A Brief Romantic Interlude" in *Post-Theory*, ed. David Bordwell and Noel Carroll (Madison: University of Wisconsin Press, 1996), pp. 434–459.
10 Mulvey, L. "Visual Pleasure and Narrative Cinema" in *Film Theory and Criticism: Introductory Readings*, ed. Leo Braudy and Marshall Cohen (New York: Oxford University Press, 1999), p. 840.
11 Eco, U. *The Limits of Interpretation* (Bloomington: Indiana University Press, 1994), p. 113.
12 Wollen, P. *Signs and Meaning in the Cinema* (Bloomington: Indiana University Press, 1972), pp. 122–123, 143.
13 Genette, G. *Paratexts: Thresholds of Interpretation* (New York: Cambridge University Press, 2001).
14 Waggoner, B. *The Sagas of Ragnar Lodbrok* (New Haven: Troth Publications, 2009).
15 Landau, S. "Das Intro als eigenständige Erzählform. Eine Typologie." *Journal of Serial Narration on Television*, Vol. 1, no. 1, Spring 2013, pp. 33–36.
16 "Vikings Title Sequence by Rama Allen." *Title Design Project: The Best of Title Sequences*, http://www.titledesignproject.com/2013/11/vikings-title-sequence-by-rama-allen/ accessed February 10, 2014.
17 "Vikings." *Forget the Film, Watch the Titles*, http://www.watchthetitles.com/articles/00278-Vikings accessed February 10, 2014.
18 Landau, S. "Das Intro als eigenständige Erzählform. Eine Typologie." *Journal of Serial Narration on Television*, Vol. 1, no. 1, Spring 2013, pp. 33–36.

3

The transformation from text superimposed over an unconnected background image in the *figure–ground mode* into the linked relationship of the *calligram mode* depends on an audience recognition of a seemingly direct, immanent connection between the text and image. This link is the product of a formal structure that exploits conventions familiar from children's picture books: an image of an object, such as an apple, is accompanied by a short, declarative text in the manner of a caption—a word stating "APPLE"—identifying that object. This pairing of word::image is the *calligram*: the text shifts meaning following its identification as being a "label." Books containing calligrams are used to teach reading to children because they enable the association of the depiction with corresponding words, drawing the text and image into an intimate relationship where those words and images become interchangeable; the same morphology of text–image reappears as captions, labels or legends placed beneath images reproduced in books not directed towards children. The almost instantaneous connection and linkage of image to text, learned from these elementary readers defines this particular mode. Text and image have a mutually reinforcing relationship; their use in title sequences is familiar from static compositions employed in graphic design. Yet, the form of all these designs is constant—the text typically appears with the image it identifies. The shifts between figure–ground and calligram modes are easily understood and recognized by their viewers, and these modes often appear as different title cards comingled within the same title sequence.

The shift from independent text superimposed over a background to converging text and background requires a recognition that text and image are mutually corresponding illustrations of the same idea, enabling (and conventionally requiring) the confusion of the text presented with the imagery that accompanies it. Michel Foucault theorizes the calligram in his book *This is Not a Pipe*, a discussion of dynamics between text and image in Surrealist painter Rene Magritte's works. His analysis identifies the calligram as a complex first-level recognition: since the image functions as an immediately understood illustration of language, it is a common feature of title cards where footage of an actor has their name superimposed along with their portrait. The text–image articulation is a duality: the image and the text do not compete for the audience's attention, but function as a singular unit; in titles, this linkage of depiction and language reiterates the caption or legend, where text apparently explains image. This text–image composite shifts around telling::showing, linking the image and the text directly. The title card illustrates a singular idea, as Foucault notes, conventionally requiring the confusion of the text presented with the imagery that accompanies it. This linkage defines the calligram. The ambiguities surrounding combinations of text and image create complex networks of identification and illustration that serve to establish and affirm specific identities existing *a priori* to their invocation:

> The calligram aspires playfully to efface the oldest oppositions of our alphabetical civilization: to show and to name; to shape and to say; to reproduce and to articulate; to imitate and to signify; to look and to read. Pursuing its quarry by two paths, the calligram sets the most perfect trap. By its double formation, it guarantees capture, as neither discourse alone, nor a pure drawing could do.[1]

The dynamic of reading::seeing Foucault describes is an opposition that subordinates image to word. This process of enculturation begins in childhood since the calligram and its structure of image and text are commonly employed in elementary readers for young children. It is ironic that this oldest opposition also appears in the most basic, often first books children encounter: it is from this experience that the subordination of image to word is learned because the enculturation produced by the calligram is one where language comes to dominate the images it accompanies. This ordering function reflects Foucault's understanding of optics as a structuring of the world, one that subordinates image to language. In the calligram language comes to dominate the images it accompanies, because the text–image pairing implies they are interchangeable, enabling them to act as doubles for each other, in the process teaching their connection as a function of lexical relationship—the name of the fruit, the word 'APPLE,' and an image depicting that same fruit converge—and the morphology of design, where the proximity and placement of text-to-image creates the form used in children's books in the title sequences for motion pictures.

Calligrams link actors with their visage, assigning and inscribing the actor's identity onto their image in a specific film. *The Big Broadcast of 1937* (Paramount, 1936) is a paradigmatic example of the hierarchical dimensions that Foucault has noted about the calligram. Asserting order (language) as the dominant dimension of the calligram establishes the boundaries of comprehension—the limits of interpretive and conceptual possibility. The duality of the calligram, then, functions to reiterate what Foucault has identified as the "empirical gaze": this unified paradigm is an actively engaged, organizational process that imposes order where there had been uncertainty. Vision assumes a privileged position in the translation of visual experience into the knowledge contained by language.

Vision embodies Foucault's concept of power: authority is enforced by language, and performed *as* reading: in the calligram mode, this linkage of connotation (language) and depiction (image) occupies a privileged place in relation to vision as a dominant, ordering system precisely because it simultaneously embodies the dualistic engagement of reading::seeing. Thus, the calligram is subversive of this hierarchy (it confuses the image and the text), and a guarantee of its ordering (it forces both elements into a mutually dependent assertion of coincident meaning). The validity of the calligram depends on the correspondence of the image to the text that accompanies it, producing an empirical demonstration of mutually corresponding associations via depicted image and text that provides a name *for* that image.

The Calligram Mode

The stills in Figure 3.1 from the uncredited design for *The Big Broadcast of 1937* reveal a title sequence that makes extensive use of calligrams: the performers are all identified through this connection of text–image, accompanied by a voice-over reinforcing the connection shown visually. The use of calligrams in *The Big Broadcast of 1937* matches the purpose of this film generally: to establish radio stars—known for the sound of their voices—as motion picture stars. The calligram's linkage of actors to their names gives a face (image) to already familiar voices. Because this film is a *star vehicle* for comedians who already had established themselves on radio, it transitions them from the audio-only world of radio shows to the audio-visual world of motion pictures. Produced as a follow-up to *The Big Broadcast of 1936* (Paramount, 1935) and employing the same cast of radio show comedians, this title sequence uses the same production techniques typical of other Paramount pictures during the 1930s—live action with optically printed type, allowing a fusion of live action photography with composited text. An almost identical title design to *The Big Broadcast of 1937* appears three years earlier in *She Done Him Wrong* (Paramount, 1933) where the actors appear "as" their characters; however, unlike the earlier sequence from 1933, which contains only twelve title cards that dissolve into each other, *The Big Broadcast of 1936* has a total of twenty title cards, and employs

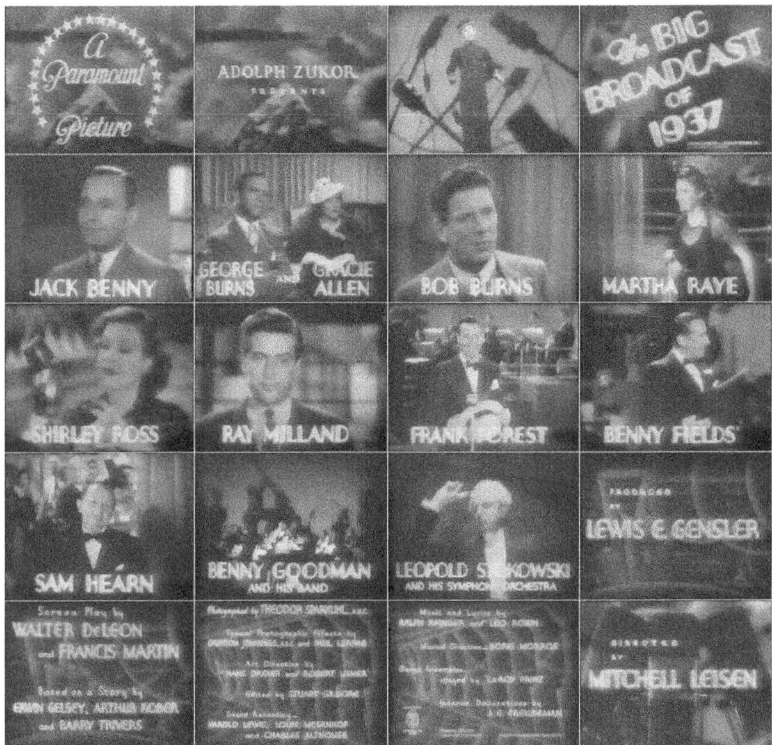

Figure 3.1 All the title cards in *The Big Broadcast of 1937* (Paramount, 1936)

optically printed transitions to suggest pages turning, making it an unusually long and complex title sequence.

Title sequences in Hollywood films of the 1930s always follow the same progression of discrete elements, located at the very beginning of the film. This ordering is retained even in much later decades: first is the production company logo. The statement "A Paramount Picture" is superimposed over a painting of a mountain; the fanfare swells and this logo dissolves into a title stating "Adolph Zukor Presents." These opening title cards are a common feature of Paramount productions. This initial logo dissolves into the particular title sequence for *The Big Broadcast of 1937*, which is composed from live action shots. The sequence starts with a giant microphone shadow looming over a child dressed as an usher who comes forward, yelling at the audience through clenched teeth and gesturing for silence: "*Quiet! Quiet! Quiet! We're on the air!*" Cut to an extreme close-up of a male face in partial profile speaking into a microphone while text appears diagonally on-screen in synchronization with his words: "The Big Broadcast of 1937." This text and the remaining title cards have been optically printed to create the effect of an animated picture book; each title card 'folds' into view, as if a page is being turned, entering the screen dynamically from alternating sides of the screen while the same voice announces the actor's identity shown in the superimposed text on-screen. This connection helps establish their identities as "stars," and reinforces the performer's title cards as *specifically* calligrams: these title cards' naming of the various actors appearing in the film function as identifying captions, while the other title cards that come both before and after these actor credits employ the figure–ground mode.

The announcer introduces the stars appearing in the film, starting with "Jack Benny," a familiar narrative convention taken from the radio programs that featured these same actors. This conventional *radio program* opening serves a double purpose: to establish the narrative space as being that of a radio station preparing to do a "big broadcast," and to link the start of the fictional story about that radio station to the design of the title sequence itself. The calligrams have the same morphology across all ten title cards, with each star appearing as they are named: "Jack Benny" is followed by "George Burns and Gracie Allen"; then "Bob Burns"; "Martha Raye"; "Ray Milland"; "Frank Forrest"; "Benny Fields"; "Sam Hearn"; "Benny Goodman and his Band"; "Leopold Stokowski and his Symphony Orchestra." The morphology of these star's title cards and the associated photographic portrait (background to the text) reproduces the formal structure of the calligram equally in all these title cards. Each of these title cards employs a design that follows the same consistent format of live action images 'folding' into view from alternating places on the right and left, before dissolving into the concluding section, where the mode shifts to the more common figure–ground mode for the final five title cards containing production credits superimposed over a graphic background and accompanied by the sequence's background music. The last five title cards are visibly unlike the earlier calligrams: none of them appear over a live action photograph, the announcer does not read their contents, nor do they suggest an illustrative linkage between the text and the background image.

The structure of this title sequence, with its synchronization of announced name, photograph of actor, and optically printed caption works to both assert the calligramic organization of these materials, and establishes the relationship of these titles to what follows through the boy's announcement that "we're on the air"—that the show has started. The artificiality of this convention from radio being transferred to film is repeated by the obviously fabricated nature of the title sequence as a whole—while the film takes place in a radio studio, at the same time it is *not* a radio program and not limited by the constraints of being "live" as radio was. Unlike the necessarily after-the-fact recording of motion pictures, the world of radio performance in the 1930s was one centered around live performance, done in simultaneous time to that of its audience listening. The titles for *The Big Broadcast of 1937* thus act as an intermediary between the fictional space of the story and the reality of the actors performing, and on a second level for its audience of 1936, intermediating the shift of these actors from radio to film. The choice of designing them as calligrams therefore reiterates the authoritarian function of the gaze that is the focus of Foucault's analysis: the connection of text–image works to assign a specific image to a particular, already-known, comedian. The authority assumed in this linkage is an inherent dimension of the calligram itself, a fundamental part of how this formal structure generates an apparently empirical, descriptive connection between photograph and caption.

In assuming an external, presentational role as identification of each actor in turn, all title cards using the calligram mode function in an identical manner. The first of these calligrams in *The Big Broadcast of 1937* shows the actor Jack Benny looking off screen to the left and silently talking to someone unseen; at the bottom of the frame are the words "Jack Benny" accompanied by the announcer's voice-over stating "with Jack Benny." The linkage of text (both written and spoken) to image seems obvious, inevitable. However, in order to make the image-text link, the audience must both look at the image and read the words—and then arrive at a correlation of both actions. The image shows *Jack Benny*, and both the voice-over and caption assert that this link is the appropriate one to make; the sound in this design is redundant, unnecessary to make the link between text and image. Even without sound, the connection of text–image emerges as an illustrative declaration; however obvious this connection might appear, it is the assumption of *inevitability* which is problematic, as Foucault explains:

> The calligram never speaks and represents at the same moment. The very thing that is both seen and read is hushed in the vision, hidden in the reading.[2]

Reading and seeing are two different activities, requiring very different kinds of conceptual and intellectual engagement. They occupy distinct spheres of engagement and knowledge. This shifting relationship between language and embodied vision is central to Foucault's critique of knowledge: in seeing the picture, we do not read the text, but in reading the text, the image necessarily becomes secondary, an illustration of the text, rendering the picture an informational addendum. Because the text is at once both simultaneously a part of the image shown on-screen, and at the same time, fundamentally *detached* from it—the words "Jack Benny" are superimposed, burned-in through overexposure, to create a clear white space in the black–and-white film that projects this title card, not a part of the visual space nor understood to be a part of it by the audience. The organization of this single title card evokes the schema already established by the children's reader where the image is identified by words placed beneath it. The conventional role of calligrams as captions or labels accompanying images in books and newspapers combines with the immanent encounter with the film to assert the linkage of text and image: thus the seen image is silenced by the act of reading (much as Benny himself silently mouths words to an unseen, absent addressee). This process reifies the dynamic of reading::seeing as a dual articulation, converging rather than parallel as in the figure–ground mode, demonstrating Foucault's conception of language dominating the gaze as order-generating authority.

The linkage of text::image (or text::speech) is immediately understood by the viewer who fluently identifies how to engage the calligram mode, masking the complex dynamics of text and image structures producing the apparently immediate linkage. In seeing the apparent relationship between name and live action photography, the audience understands that this text is presented as a label—an identifier—and thus an instance of a calligram; the figure–ground mode placements in the sequence do not produce such an immediate connection, precisely because the calligram subordinates text to image, producing an immediate recognition of a formal relation between text-that-names and image-which-shows: it is a mutually reinforcing illustration. The calligram renders the connection of reading::seeing through a logic of similarity and duplicitous naming/showing. The information provided by the text is simultaneously redundant—the person shown is Jack Benny, and at the same time is a necessary illustration since the film is a work of fiction, and that while the person shown *is* Jack Benny, within the diegesis of the film, he *is* "Jack Carson," someone else entirely, an imaginary character who is represented (played) by Jack Benny within the story. The interrelationship of text as legend or caption, and the image as illustration or demonstration—the essential form posed by the calligram—is a conventional one, and it gives the title cards their apparent clarity. It is not yet apparent that "Jack Benny" who is both named by the voice-over and labeled by the text is to be called "Jack Carson," nor is it certain that this silent image will later speak within the film, answering to a different name and advancing the pretense that it is not standing before a camera, being filmed—that it is not part of a fictional production assembled from various shots each produced independently of the others, at different times and not necessarily in the sequence shown.

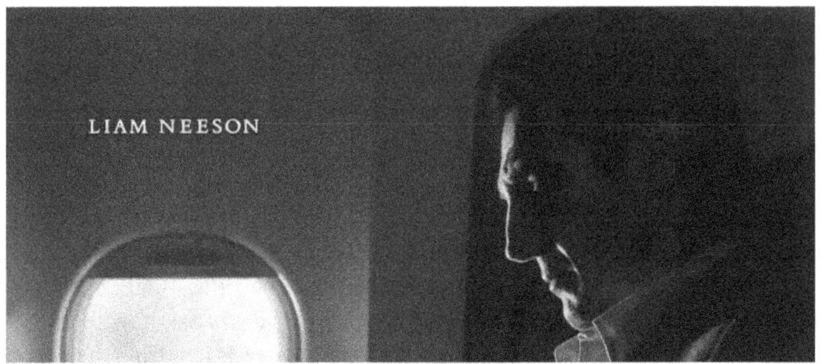

Figure 3.2 A calligram title card stating "Liam Neeson" from *Unknown* (2011)

The title design for *Unknown* (2011) reiterates these same problematics of naming and performance—*reading::seeing*—common to the calligram. Just as with Jack Benny, this calligram functions to provide a real identity for the actor whose performance will be as someone else entirely. A live action shot of Liam Neeson at an airplane window is simultaneously accompanied by the words "Liam Neeson" appearing next to his head [Figure 3.2]; the linkage of text–image is immediately clear: Liam Neeson the actor simultaneously appears on-screen, identified and labeled by the text "Liam Neeson." This placement is important. It facilitates the audience recognition of it as a "label" identifying this man as the actor, connecting his name to the character he plays on-screen. Yet the audience knows before the film begins that this relationship, as with "Jack Benny" in 1936 [Figure 2.2], is one where the character and the actor *will* diverge. In *Unknown*, this linkage is complicated by the merging of title sequence with dramatic narrative: "Liam Neeson" sitting by an airplane window is the beginning of the story, the title card merges with this fictional world. The title sequence occupies a special position in relation to that 'world,' a part of it and simultaneously absent from it; such ambiguity of linkage increases the uncertainty of the relationship between the title and the image: located at the interface between the 'outside' and the 'inside' of the narrative. The problems evoked by both these presentations raise questions about the reality of what appears on-screen that Douglas P. Lackey has discussed in his critique of Stanley Cavell's ontological study of motion pictures, *The World Viewed*:

> Is it true that standard films represent reality in such a way that we must accept their subjects as having a reality independently of the films

> in which they appear? The proper answer is that it all depends. If you are dealing with a still photograph, you are compelled almost always to treat it as a document; a photograph of Jones represents Jones as he really was, at some place and some time. But if you have a feature film, in which the actors have roles, then there is no longer any compulsion to accept what is seen as real.[3]

The contradiction between showing and naming is the problem of realism that Lackey identifies. When there is a self-contained, independent title sequence, it only emerges later in the film after the titles—once the story actually begins. But these questions never arise: We *can* ask how to understand the relationship of "Jack Benny" to their image (drawn from the action of the film) showing "Jack Carson" *who* is portrayed by the radio star Jack Benny? We understand that *of course* Jack Benny the actor-comedian is only performing a role in the film that follows, that the "Jack Benny" of the title card will answer to another name in the narrative.

In the opening to *Unknown*, what relationship does this label stating "Liam Neeson" have to the story that has already begun? For *Unknown*, a film about a man who arrives in Paris only to be replaced by another man, the opening label asserting his identity-as-actor takes on a humorous dimension: *of course* his identity will be "stolen"—it is only a role he plays in a film! A joke the audience can only recognize in retrospect. The conventional nature of this opening hides the title's joke about identities—"Liam Neeson" will spend the narrative insisting that his name is that of the character, yet we know this is all a performance, all a fiction. His real name, true name is entirely different and all the attempts to assert otherwise are doomed from the beginning by this calligramic identification—how could it be otherwise? Yet these relationships creating this joke disappear precisely because to acknowledge them puts the drama into question, rupturing the realism of its presentation. They only become apparent in the abstract consideration separate from what transpires in the film itself—we must ignore the paratextual relationship of title to narrative and consider instead this opening as an autonomous, reflexive engagement with its own form, a critical rejection of the as-yet unseen story for this joke to reveal itself.

Unlike theater—where the reality of the actors remains a constant feature of their performance and the audience occupies a fixed position (single vantage point)—in motion pictures the actors are simultaneously visible and absent, and because of the dynamic space potentially available through editing and the conventions of cinematic mimesis, the limited point of view common to theater is replaced by the cinematic view of the camera; the artifice of cinematic realism conceals the actual production process. The use of calligrams in title sequences to link actors with their real-world names thus serves an essential function in commercializing cinema through the identification of the "star" independently of the role played. However, the order imposed by the calligram remains problematic specifically because of the difference between the ontological reality of the actors pretending to be (mimesis) and the epistemological ambiguity of the mismatch between the naming shown in the title sequence and the different naming used in the film's narrative: for motion pictures, unlike other kinds of theater, have the capacity to produce an illusion that what is shown on (in) the screen is an independent world, other than and separate from the one the audience inhabits (as Stanley Cavell has noted in his book *The World Viewed*). It is at the same time an acknowledgment of the fictitious nature of the commercial narrative film: the name that the actor responds to on-screen is not their own; the calligram mode counteracts this effacement of identity by inscribing the "true identity" of the actors onto their images, contradicting the fictional name they use within the film narrative. This formal device always must subordinate image to language: the dominant function of a calligram is to establish the boundaries of comprehension—the limits of interpretive and conceptual understanding; in the case of a title sequence, this is the distinction between actor and character. The "joke" in *Unknown* then becomes a critical commentary on the nature of title sequences and their inherent contradiction of all that is fictional in the film that follows. In producing these distinctions—superimposed text as non-diegetic, external to the "reality" on-screen—it reiterates the enclosed, independent nature of the narrative fiction through (paradoxically) instructing the audience in the real identity of the actor as distinguished from the character being portrayed, making the fiction apparent as such.

This opposition of reality and fiction reiterates Foucault's understanding of the calligram as a formal structure. In demonstrating the active organization created by the clinical gaze, it imposes order through a translation of visual experience into the knowledge contained by language. Sight is an actively engaged, organizational process that renders the world as this hierarchy in which vision is its central directive force. Thus, the calligram is privileged since it embodies a paradoxical duality that is both subversive of the hierarchy it produces (it confuses the image with the text), and an assertion of the ordering principles that make the hierarchy possible (it combines text and image into a mutually dependent relationship asserting what appears to be a singular meaning). It functions as an empirical naming of the object depicted, and in doing so works against the abstract character of language itself specifically through this simultaneous presentation and announcement of what is presented, revealing the contradictory nature of the calligram mode employed in *The Big Broadcast of 1937*. The content of the image and the meaning of the text are identical—it is their reflexive similarity that provides the apparently empirical statement of "fact" as well as invokes Foucault's specifically clinical gaze. This duality is reiterated throughout Hollywood's films first as the star and then again through the conventions of cinematic realism. Both of these acts are empirical, a clinical function of the gaze that imposes order instantaneously via the calligram's conventional link of depiction to language. The audience is complicit in the doubling, aware that what appears on film and what is reality are not the same, but have been organized to achieve a reality-effect. Unlike the figure–ground mode, the calligram mode asserts this empirical connection between the depiction and the text, one that serves important commercial functions beyond those of narrative in *The Big Broadcast of 1936* by linking the established radio star "Jack Benny" with the to-be-established film star "Jack Benny"—in doing so, the function of calligramic titles makes the paradoxical nature of the *role* apparent. For "Liam Neeson," it is the maintenance of his identity that the calligram mode reaffirms by attaching his name to his image, even as the narrative in *Unknown* will disassociate the two. The limitations of cinematic storytelling—the flatness of the space, those structures employed in editing, the inclusion of mood music—that are different from actual lived experience are *expected* in the film world.

In the traditional conception of a title sequence where each card acts to introduce the fictional world of the film, this empirical relationship becomes problematic: the calligram mode asserts the reality distinguished from the drama. The complexity and contradiction of the relationship between text and image becomes apparent once the film drama begins: Liam Neeson is not called "Liam Neeson" in *Unknown*, nor is the man shown in *The Big Broadcast of 1937* called "Jack Benny"—the actors credited in the titles of fiction films are not the same as the characters they portray, and the audience is never confused by this mismatch—it is a foundational convention of theatrical narratives that the actors who appear on-screen are playing a role, different and distinct from their identities when *not* playing that role in the motion picture. Everything named in the calligram mode is on view, conventionally presenting a coincident instruction of both the image's name and the text's denoted meaning. The title sequence enacts a contradiction attenuated by the conventional nature of *acting* itself—that the actor and the role coincide in film but at the same moment remain distinct—buttressed by the "star system" operative in Hollywood's productions, and which both *Unknown* and *The Big Broadcast of 1937* specifically employ: these actors are "stars," their recognition by the audience is expected—anticipated—by their presentation in the title design. The authority posed by the "star system" and the demands of the fiction doubles the relationship of reality to character even before the calligram mode poses it through the combination of superimposed text and photographic image. These dynamics, however complex, are also quotidian, familiar, a recurrent part of the title design as such.

The "Cut Scene" Montage

The use of "cut scenes" in television title sequences are calligrams, but replace the singular image common to the feature film title design with a series of vignettes that construct a portrait of the actor(s) central to the program, a serial form where the variations created by different performance-images combine as a composite portrait.[4] When "cut scene" montages do appear in feature film title sequences, as with the main-on-end design for *Iron Man 3* (2013) by Danny Yount, the design evokes TV precisely because this approach is rare in feature film sequences, and common on television. Serial calligrams offer a complex portrait demonstrating what and how the actor presents their role: this type of title design is constructed from shots selected from those appearing in the program, and when they are accompanied by the actor's superimposed name, become a more complex variant of the calligrams familiar from feature films. In place of a singular image, these vignettes often show isolated moments in rapid succession; in some titles, the text overlays the entire sequence, in others it only appears at the end of each actor's sequence as a final identifier, a summation of *who* the actor is. Montage creates a variant of the typical calligram, distributing the relationship of text::image across a multiple of images, rather than isolating just one image directly. In this arrangement of moments, what becomes clear is the *constancy* of performance, allowing the audience to recognize the same actor pass through a range of moods and appearances.

In the cut-scene montage, the quotational nature of the selected parts is anticipatory, a reversal of the typical play of serial quotations, that when rendered as a calligram invites a consideration of other features than the narrative function of these scenes: it does not matter if the audience already knows them or not, since their presence is transformed by the calligram mode. These extractions draw attention to the qualities and nuances of the acting, its performative dimension apart from its narrative or dramatic characters, so when encountered later, the audience can focus on the drama instead of *how* it is performed.

Television mystery-drama *Magnum, P.I.* (CBS, 1980–1988) ran for eight seasons, each new season accompanied by a title sequence "refresh" that updated its contents; the first season, however, had three distinct title sequences, each with their own organization and changed theme music: all three versions were produced at Universal Title, but while no designer is credited, the composer is. The familiar music by Mike Post, used as the main theme for seven seasons, was only introduced in episode 12 of season

1 as a redesign of the title sequence that introduced the familiar theme music along with major changes to the cut-scene montage. This third variation of the opening runs 60 seconds and contains four individual sequences, one per main character, each ending with a superimposed title credit. The structure of this montage is linear. The title character, "Magnum" played by Tom Selleck, appears first [Figure 3.3] in eight shots showing him performing a variety

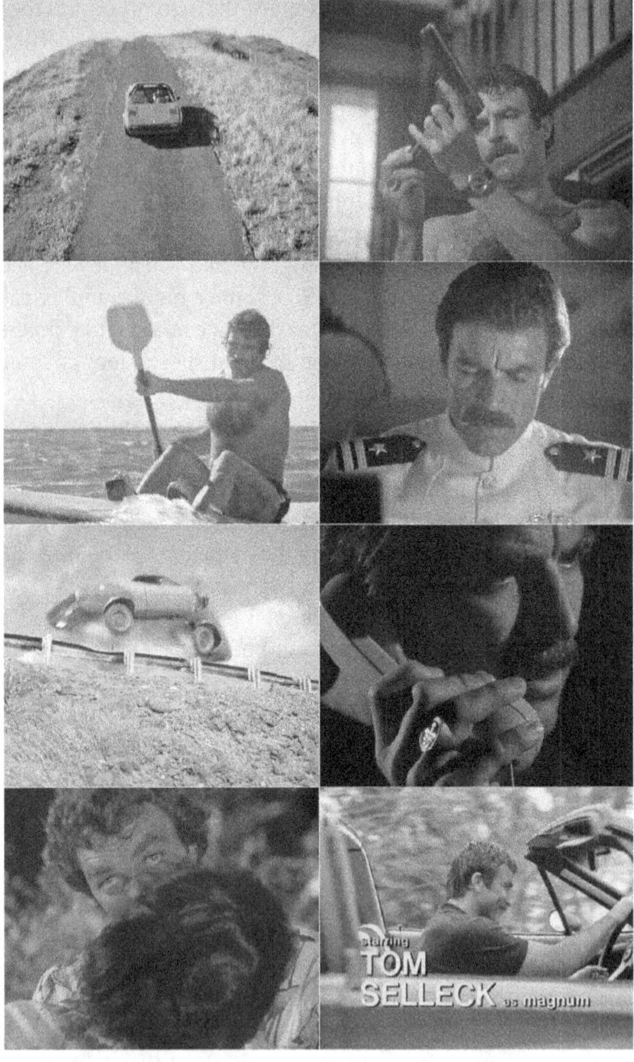

Figure 3.3 Cut-scene montage for Tom Selleck from *Magnum P.I.* (season 1, 1980)

of actions. His is the most varied and dynamic series: it is a double-length version of the structure used for his co-stars. Following this first sequence, there are two transition shots between each co-star, then a two-person shot where they appear interacting with Selleck's character "Magnum," and then each secondary character/actor appears alone in three additional shots performing an action reflective of their role in the series. John Hillerman, who plays "Higgins" [Figure 3.4], comes first. The end of Selleck's sequence acts as transition; Hillerman's sequence portrays "Higgins" as a haughty, pompous 'Brit' who is vaguely at odds with Magnum. He takes a decanter away from Magnum, practices martial arts, then (in a low-angle shot) looks down in disdain. The transition is a shot of the helicopter from the start of the titles, followed by a view from inside as it speeds over the coast. This transition introduces Roger E. Mosley, who plays "T.C." [Figure 3.5]. His role is as Magnum's pilot; he flies the helicopter while Magnum uses a camera to photograph something on the ground. This shot is followed by T.C. laughing, inspecting a bullet casing, and finally reclining while seated at his desk. Larry Manetti, who plays "Rick" [Figure 3.6], appears as 'comic

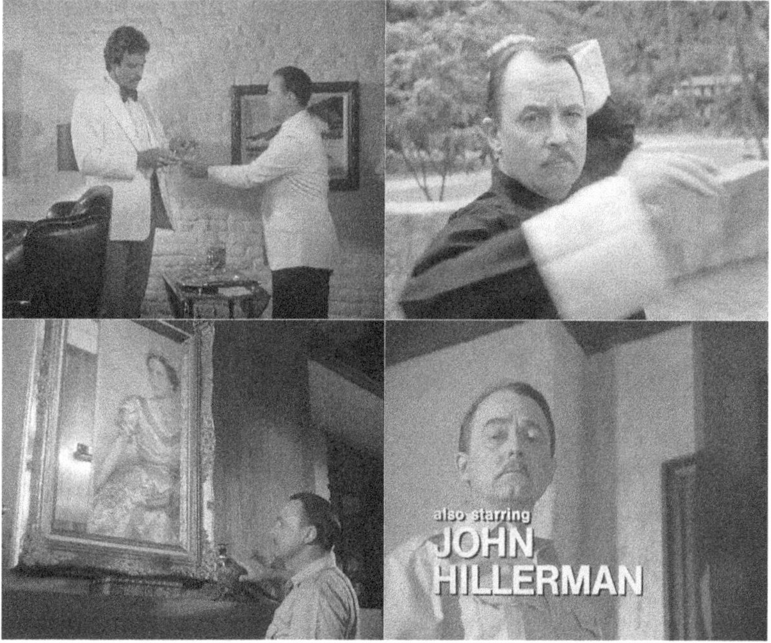

Figure 3.4 Cut-scene montage for John Hillerman from *Magnum P.I.* (season 1, 1980)

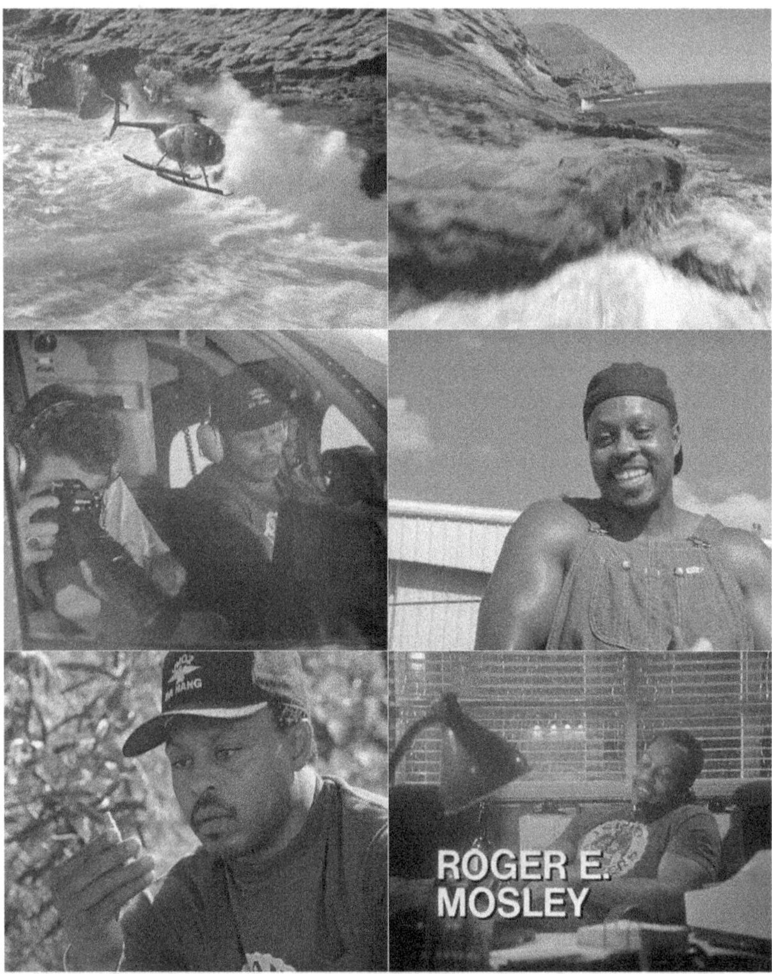

Figure 3.5 Cut-scene montage for Roger E. Mosley from *Magnum P.I.* (season 1, 1980)

relief.' His montage is the mirror-image of "Higgins"—"Rick" is a buffoon: he rides in the red Ferrari while Magnum drives, leans against the edge of a swimming pool wearing a mask and snorkel, flips a switch while dressed in a polka-dot outfit, and says something while wearing a straw hat. These co-star vignettes all follow the same pattern: each of these four-shot montages produces a portrait of the character where the actor's and character's name are both identified at the sequence's conclusion via a superimposed title

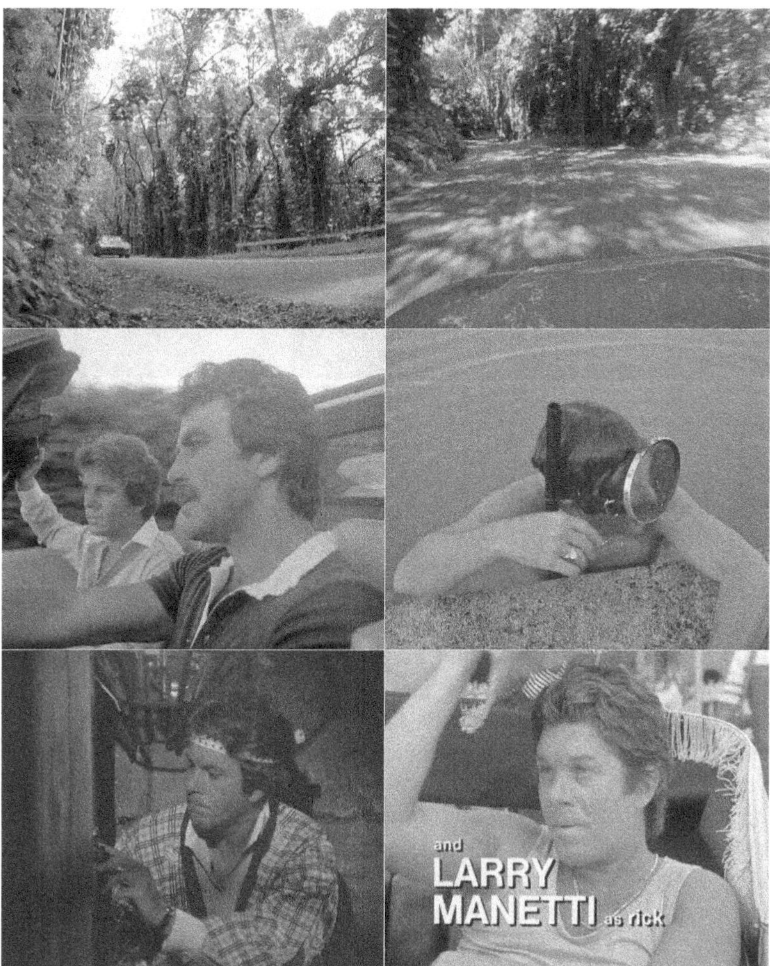

Figure 3.6 Cut-scene montage for Larry Manetti from *Magnum P.I.* (season 1, 1980)

card. It is an adaptation of the same formal device commonly used since the 1910s to introduce individual characters/actors in feature films [Figure 3.7].

The summative aspect of these cut-scene montages is specifically illustrative. The calligram mode acts as punctuation, identifying the conclusion of each portrait. It 'ends' the series, allowing the next to begin. Shifting between one illustrative serial and the next comes through the linking shots that identify the character's relationship to Magnum: for "Higgins," this

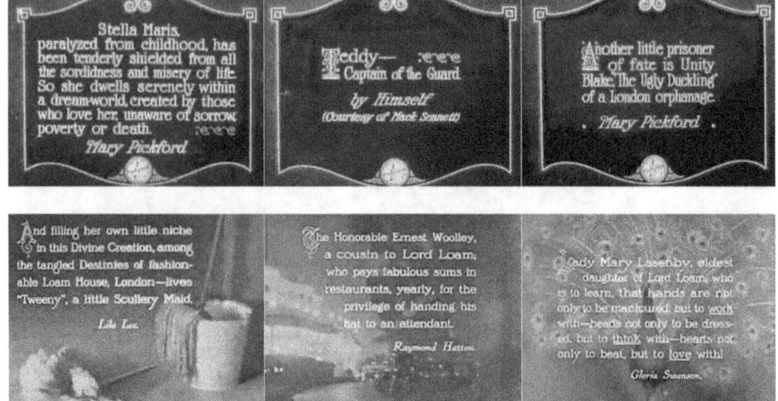

Figure 3.7 Title cards introducing actors with narrative descriptions of their character
TOP: from *Stella Maris* (Artcraft Pictures, 1918)
BOTTOM: from *Male and Female* (Paramount, 1919)

connection comes at the end when the red Ferrari drives away. The subsequent groups for "T.C." and "Rick" establish this relationship through the contextual provided by the paired shots at each vignette's beginning. In all three co-star sequences, this structure implies a narrative connection that the entire opening title is designed to provide: it tells the audience who these characters are in relation to the titular *Magnum, P.I.* The calligram mode extends throughout each sequence—even though the superimposed text only appears at the end, it is expected, anticipated, by the audience, who immediately grasp this opening as a *narrative* explanation of the characters being introduced, comparable to the descriptive texts shown in Figure 3.7. The separation between title card and photographic illustration is irrelevant to the audience's recognition and interpretation of this organization. Each shot in the montage functioning as an elemental portrait that "adds up" to the superimposed text at the end—the entire series of shots *is* the calligram emerging over time: an illustration-in-time that renders the images redundant to the text. The duplicity of the title cards—the actor and the role are both identified—coupled with the images establish them as converging, complementary elements that the montage has displaced throughout the group of shots on display.

The separation of live actor from fictional role presented/constructed in the film is governed by a set of conventions not least of which is the framing and staging of the film itself to hide and render invisible all the techniques required for its production. The final shot of the *Magnum P.I.* title sequence reveals this conventional nature: the actor Tom Selleck, as "Magnum," turns and looks into the camera in a direct address to the audience, comically raising his eyebrows, thus acknowledging what the audience already knows: the pleasures and attractions of the mimetic realism employed in Hollywood films emerge from a provisional acceptance of the fictional "world" introduced in the title montage. The dualities of title cards naming the actors in conjunction with their image on-screen is part of this conventionalized realism, where instead of rupturing the illusion, it draws attention to it as such, as a construct, allowing the audience to acknowledge its functionality in a complicit, knowing fashion.

The title sequence is self-evidently artificial, but at the same time, visibly stylized, making its artificiality both the focus and content of its production; for the audience watching the titles, they are aware of this interplay between telling::showing, reading::looking. The shifting figure–ground and calligram modes that structure title sequences demonstrate how the audience understands the titles as an introduction to the actors and simultaneously preparing for the narrative that follows. The shifting perceptual modes of reading::looking are accompanied by a shifting of relationships—the "suspension of disbelief"—to accept that the diegesis on film is its own world, separate from ours. These shifts depend on the distinction between real names and dramatic roles that marks the boundary of the fictional realm within the production itself.

Documentary Realism

The realism of fiction productions depends on a distinction between actuality and fictional construct that the calligram mode serves to affirm through the different identities of performance and actor. In documentary productions, the calligram mode functions as a demonstration of the same convergence, but without the distinction of identities specific to fiction: in documentaries, the person identified and their identity-role are the same. For documentary designs, that the calligram hides the duality of denotative image and connotative text as an apparently natural, automatic convergence is an essential part of how these productions establish themselves as "factual." The calligram asserts an established order imposed through reading as a force evacuating the conventional nature of these relations *as* the "transparency" of photography-typography composited into a singular unit, the title card itself. It is this linkage of text-to-image the calligram provides, the certainty of that connection, that is important to its use in documentary productions. This unity gives the mode its annunciative power and immediacy of effect. In rendering its conventional association—as in fiction titles where the connection of text naming "Liam Neeson" or "Jack Benny" to their image—the calligram mode also substantiates the realism of the film's presentation. It enables the audience's certainty that when these actors appear in the drama, they will answer to another, different name that may have no relation to their actual identity. The realism of the depiction and the reality of the association assert the fictional nature of the story through their marked difference from it. Because the fictional world shown by the narrative is not identical to the naming provided by the title cards, it becomes all the more secure in its conventional "reality." This function allows what Richard Rushton has described as the "forms of life" approach to realism shared by Stanley Cavell and André Bazin, where "knowledge is about a social understanding of reality, intersubjective acknowledgements about what should or can be decided upon as real."[5] The calligram's assertion of a truthful presentation of facts that act in contradistinction to the fictional performance grants both positions a degree of stability since both fiction and fact depend on a conscious identification of *how* the motion picture resembles: for the audience to mistake the fiction of the film for a documentary reality *outside* that production requires a confusion about the nature of realism and reality. This separation is the duality of the mode itself; the calligram provides an identification, but it also inscribes the difference between media presentation and reality directly into the production through the social role of audience recognition and acknowledgment of the mediated production that the calligram enables.

Thus, calligrams are employed with greater insistence in documentary productions than in fictional ones: in *Zelig* (1981) the film starts quickly. There are three brief title cards composed from white text on a black background with a total running time of approximately 20 seconds; the third of these opening titles states, "The following documentary would like to give special thanks to Dr. Eudora Fletcher, Paul Deghuee, and Mrs. Meryl Fletcher Varney" [Figure 3.8], followed quickly by what appears to be

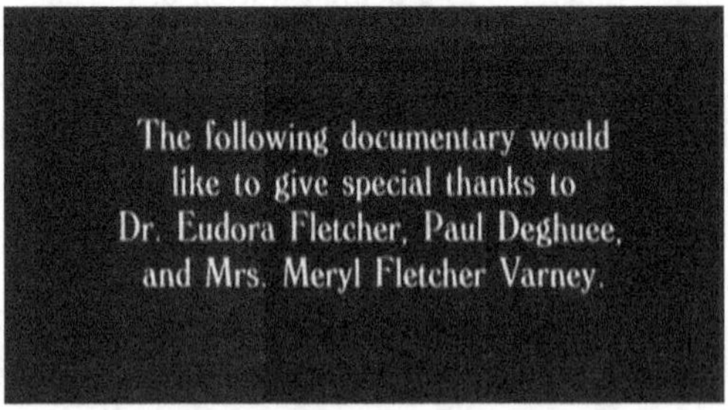

Figure 3.8 Title card stating, "The following documentary would like to give special thanks to Dr. Eudora Fletcher, Paul Deghuee, and Mrs. Meryl Fletcher Varney," from *Zelig* (1981)

newsreel footage of a parade. Thirty-six seconds into the film, a woman appears in front of a window with an indistinct scene behind her, and a moment later some text appears below her on-screen stating "Susan Sontag" [Figure 3.9]. When "Susan Sontag" appears on-screen talking about "how remarkable" the fictional Leonard Zelig was, the relationship between her name and her image align with the use of calligrams in fiction films. It is the first in a series of brief statements by people accompanied by a name: Sontag is followed by "Saul Bellow" and then by "Irving Howe." These combinations of text and image are much like how Jack Benny is accompanied by his name in *The Big Broadcast of 1937*—but with one significant difference: in *Zelig*, "Susan Sontag" is appearing in the film *as* Susan Sontag. She is presenting herself as herself in a fictional film that employs and develops from the conventions of documentary yet tells an entirely artificial (and physically impossible) historical narrative about "The Changing Man." Sontag's role in this fiction is as "Sontag"; that is, she fictionally presents herself as a fictional character she plays, an entanglement of reality::fiction, which the calligram mode reinforces through its labeling function. The full problematics of this documentary are beyond the scope of the present analysis—what is important to the current discussion is exactly this doubling of fictional and non-fictional personae where the truthful identification becomes at the same moment an invocation of a fictional reality.

The "Susan Sontag" of *Zelig* is a *fictional* critic and author whose appearance in the film, played by an actor who happens to be in her real life a critic and author named "Susan Sontag." The same relationships of fiction and performance apply to "Saul Bellow" and "Irving Howe," who also appear

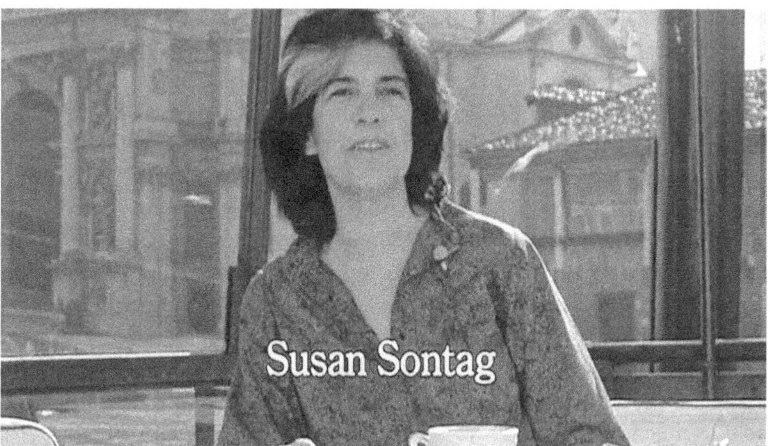

Figure 3.9 A calligram title card stating "Susan Sontag" from *Zelig* (1981)

in this sequence. The coincidence of fictional portrayal and factual identity *outside* the narrative encourages a confusion of the structured depiction with the recognitions this calligram sets in motion; this socially organized series of distinctions are what produces the enjoyment for the audience who understands the doubling and play of non/fiction. These overlaps and confusions of depiction with reality are particular to the documentary form, in fact, are its definitional condition—the audience is expected and expects to make the association of portrayal and actuality, to link the presentation with the world beyond the motion picture precisely in the ways that they don't with fictional works. The complexity of this process reveals itself through the mirror-like regression of Sontag playing at being herself: this artifice is fundamental to how documentary links its mimetic appearance to its unrepresentable object. There can be no substitution for the reality of the world; what appears in art just as much as in motion pictures is a construct linked to that reality by the tenuous connections of depiction. It is not an issue of one depiction being *more* real than another, but of the audience engaging and identifying one series of conventional links and associations as descriptive of *real* and another series as *fiction*. The calligram mode straddles these antithetical conventions, in service of both (or neither)—a product of how it acts to enforce what Foucault has identified as the clinical (empirical) functions of vision subordinated to language as a determinant of fact and knowledge.

The difference between "Liam Neeson" or "Jack Benny" and "Susan Sontag" is not linked to the calligram mode's organization of text and image as a mutually reinforcing demonstrations of "fact" or "reality," but in the presentation and self-consciousness of the audience engaging in their production. Unlike a fictional role where the actor pretends there is no camera present, Sontag is speaking to the camera, not as an aside in an otherwise fictional scene where a fictional character speaks to the audience, but directly, a speech given *for* the audience. She is aware of the camera, and the resulting performance is akin to a public lecture: aware of the audience, yet there is no pretext of an informal conversation through the (still invisible) camera as in the fictional character's side comment. This distinction is difficult to articulate because the audience immediately recognizes and understands its conventional structure: this calligram stating "Susan Sontag" is a factual identification that functions in a fictional realm asserting and marking the difference between it and the real identity of the actor, while simultaneously functioning as an acknowledgment of the reality being shown. The convergence of image and text authenticates the audience perception that what appears is *non-fiction*; but in the case of *Zelig*, this identification of documentary form with its accompanying claims to be 'of reality' are mistaken—the film is a fictional work designed to assume the form familiar from documentary productions. Its falsity renders the documentary form's social foundations and their role in the calligram mode visible, apparent in the contradictions surrounding the shifting relationship between actor and actuality.

The calligram mode aligns with this documentary effect in *Zelig* through its immediate function as a labeling of the image: it creates the same demonstrative effect that appears in the "bottom third" graphics commonly used in news broadcasts on television; by showing the name along with the visage, the calligram mode establishes itself as an immediate, definitional statement of "fact." Foucault's identification of it as a tautology is thus accurate:

> In its millennial tradition, the calligram has a triple role: to augment the alphabet, to repeat something without the aid of rhetoric, to trap things in a double cipher.[6]

The first cipher is the text that presents its content through connotation; the second one is the image itself. The third cipher, the resemblance between the image and its denoted subject, is reinforced by the lexical identification provided by the superimposed text. In making this logical connection a tangible presence on-screen, the calligram mode renders the connection made autonomously into the verification of text by image, and image by text. This mutual reinforcement serves a secondary function as the documentary effect—it establishes the authority of the subject shown by confirming their identity for the audience. "Susan Sontag" identified must also actually be Susan Sontag for the documentary effect to assert itself. Thus, this third cipher unravels in a particular way with the connection of "Susan Sontag" to herself: to recognize this calligram not as a title card, labeling its subject with her correct identity, but as a fictional association redirects these relations into a circulating loop between Sontag-herself and fictional-Sontag where at each step her identity and the calligram's labeling change their meaning. It is at once both a credit (it *is* Susan Sontag) and a fictional artifice—she is a performer in the role of "Susan Sontag" that coincides with her identity *outside* the narrative, a recognition that reverses the claim of artifice by turning the title card into a credit once more. This instability is present at all times; it is the difference between denotation and connotation, being and naming, image and text. Her testimony achieves its factual appearance through this labeling function. *She is who she appears to be*, rather than being what her appearance in this film really is: a fictional character in the drama who is always an actor performing *as* someone else. This entanglement of non/fiction around the calligram mode only emerges from the paradoxical relationships invoked by films such as *Zelig*.

As the fictionality of *Zelig* demonstrates, the convergence of Susan Sontag performing as herself in a fictional film does not alter the documentary relations this mode invokes in this relationship. Quite the contrary, the fictional statements and drama of the film depend on this convergence—not only of Sontag with her role, but of the various historical figures such as Adolf Hitler whose presence as artifacts in the film also undergo a transformation through their intersection with the fictional life of "Leonard Zelig" played by Woody Allen. The tension of fictional and non-fictional elements set in motion by these calligrams that come at the beginning of the narrative come into focus through the contradictory association of Susan Sontag, author and critic, with "Susan Sontag," author and critic claiming the factuality of what are clearly fantastic events. Foucault's recognition that the shifting modes of reading::seeing require incompatible engagements is also an identification of the audience's shifting comprehension of their entanglement with those engagements. This complexity is always an issue of audience recognition of the shifting relationship between actor and role. The recognition of documentary form in the calligram mode is precisely this marking of differences, and it is these distinctions that *Zelig* engages and confuses in telling its story, in the process affirming the centrality of the audience's interpretation of relationship to—and acknowledgment of—the external reality beyond the motion picture that is determinant of meaning for the artifice created by the composited text and image.

Notes

1 Foucault, M. *This Is Not a Pipe* (Berkeley: University of California Press, 1982), pp. 20–22.
2 Foucault, M. *This Is Not a Pipe* (Berkeley: University of California Press, 1982), p. 25.
3 Lackey, D. "Reflections on Cavell's Ontology of Film." *The Journal of Aesthetics and Art Criticism*, Vol. 32, no. 2, Winter 1973, p. 273.
4 Eco, U. *The Limits of Interpretation* (Bloomington: University of Indiana Press, 1994), p. 89.
5 Rushton, R. *The Reality of Film: Theories of Filmic Reality* (Manchester: Manchester University Press, 2011), p. 63.
6 Foucault, M. *This Is Not a Pipe* (Berkeley: University of California Press, 1982), p. 20.

4

The rebus mode, much like the lower-level calligram mode, originates with the text::image play of children's books that deploy the ambiguous form of the "rebus" or word-image puzzle. Text and image remain as independent fields (as with the figure–ground mode), but they *are* related to each other, the linkage producing an ambivalent meaning dependent on past experience, a product of their entanglement. Understanding this form requires a careful attention not just to the text itself, but to the graphic nature of that text aside from issues of lexical intelligibility or legibility: consider *Liar* created by Paul Agule in 1987 [Figure 4.1]. It is an ambigram, a type of optical illusion whose identification is uncertain—*Liar* can be interpreted to be both a written word *and* a graphic profile of a man, but not at the same time. It poises between the realms of image and text: each understanding as profile or word forces us to blot out the other potential—even if momentarily—in a shifting of relationships between reading and seeing. Inflecting the understanding of its contents acknowledges its instability. If we choose to reject the rebus's paradoxical fusion of image and text, structure and meaning, we lose the ability to recognize the 'tension' that renders the figure coherent. The identity of the "liar" is contained in the word itself—one needs only to look at the man to see it (literally) written on his face. Agule's *rebus* links initial, lowest-level interpretations of this work as either *image* or as *text* to its duplicitous transformation: conceiving it as text (connotation) disputes the equally apparent profile (denotation), while the man's profile conflicts with our *equally* present and insistent understanding of *Liar* as a series of cursive letters. Each additional "solution" oscillates between initial, lowest-level interpretations that enable either reading the text or seeing the profile, but never settles on either action; the rebus's meaning comes from this dynamic, shifting relationship.

Because the calligram and figure–ground modes are low-level organizations of text::image that demonstrate the actions of reading::seeing are mutually exclusive activities, the shift to the rebus mode is also a change

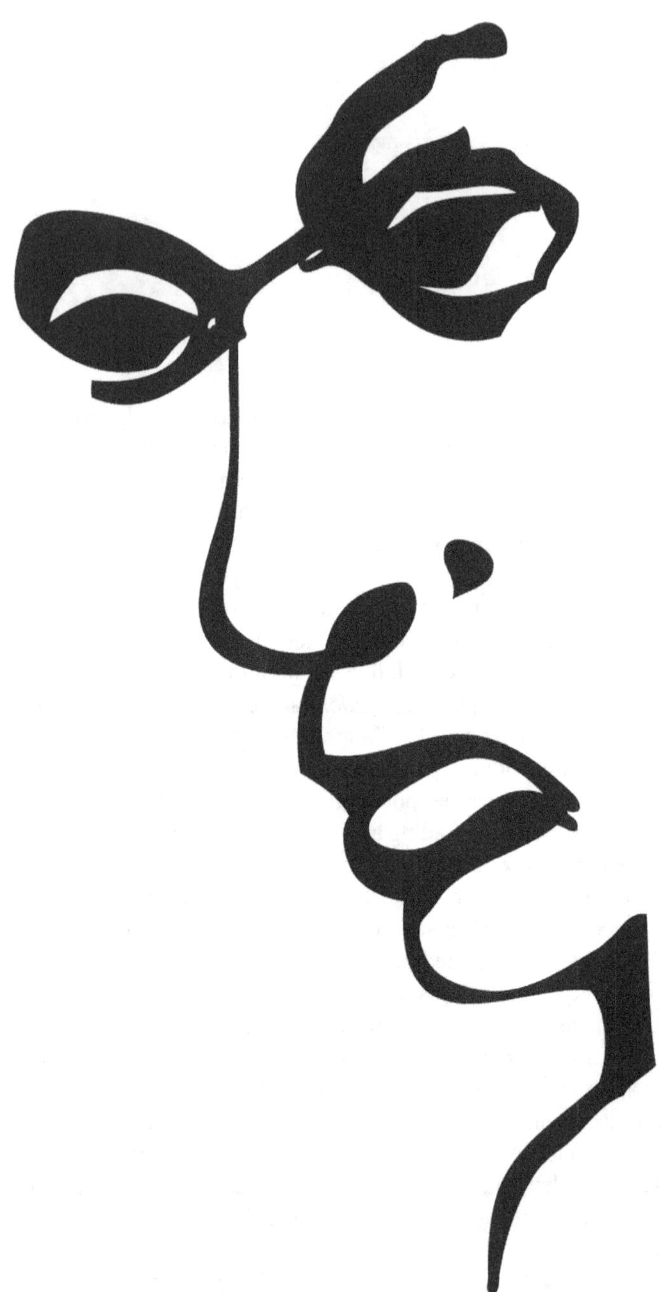

Figure 4.1 Liar ambigram by Paul Agule (1987)

in interpretive level; for the audience watching, the rhetorical inflections in all three modes act to reinforce an established (typically narrative) order through a conventional link of depiction with language: *you read the words first*. The understanding and interpretation of these modes is always transparent, easily understood—yet in being conceived as apparently natural, their relationships and complexity are masked.

What develops in the rebus mode is a structural contrast between image and typography established via rhetorical juxtapositions dependent on intertextual knowledge—such as *metonymy* and *synecdoche*—rather than via the mutually reinforcing, but independent, illustrational links of the calligram mode. These shifting roles of text and image elide the differences of reading::seeing, revealing that lexical interpretations *are* artificial, linked to lowest-level distinctions between images and words. A rebus always results from how higher-level interpretations transform lower-level oppositions: in contrast to the calligram's linkage of reading::seeing that asserts an ordered world through an immediate, apparently natural connection of text-to-image, in the juxtapositions typical of the rebus mode, the ordering produced by Foucault's 'clinical gaze' is redirected back towards itself, reveling in its artificiality. A rebus's meaning can only emerge *after* lower-level recognitions have organized the text and image, because the rebus renders these initial identifications unstable. In offering a new meaning, it presents the interpretation as a rhetorical excess, recognizable in its similarity to the additional meanings that emerge from the juxtapositions common to montage: the result is more than the sum of its parts might suggest. The rebus mode thus depends on acknowledging these arbitrary associations, on engaging the specific play that is *rhetoric*. These transformations are relatively rare in historical title sequences, a testament to the self-conscious organization required for their production. Yet, in spite of its complexity, the rebus mode is readily understood and its connections seem to appear naturally, much like the illustrative links created by the calligram mode. This immediacy renders both modes equally obvious to audiences, and obtuse when described theoretically.

Acknowledging the juxtaposition of text::image requires an interpretation to reveal its linkages and meanings in the rebus mode, and depends on the recognized but absent connections invoked through the mismatch of one term with another[1]—a rhetorical connection of text::image that is capricious rather than immanent. The shifts of *Liar* demonstrate these instabilities of identification. The implied significance created through juxtaposition of an *independent* text and image is the rhetorical process in action, immediately recognizable as both metonymy, which depends on similarity, and as synecdoche, in which a fragment symbolically stands for the whole. Juxtaposition challenges the apparent stability of lower-level interpretations through its allegorical opening of meaning into arenas whose connections are necessarily partial and indirect, drawing from the audience's past experience to recognize the imaginative (poetic) linkages offered in the rebus mode. This second-level semiological system thus stabilizes the discursive problems semiotician Roland Barthes identified as "connotation" in images—the implied meaning separate from the specifics of depiction (representation) so apparent in photography:

> Another difficulty attached to the analysis of connotation is that no particular analytic language corresponds to the particularity of its signifieds . . . they constitute within the total image *discontinuous features* or better still, *erratic features*. The connotators do not fill the entire lexia; reading them does not exhaust it. In other words (and this would be a proposition valid for semiology in general), all the elements of the lexia cannot be transformed into connotators.[2]

The instability of connotation when addressed as a single system—text or image—creates the appearance of a controlled, fixed meaning through the calligram; this apparent limitation of meaning recovers its basic ambiguity through the juxtaposition of text::image inherent to the rebus. Issues of depiction versus connotation provide an implicit foundation for the shift between interpretive levels: depiction is a necessary feature of those interpretations arising from the combination of text–image; second-level interpretations depend on the ambiguity of connotation—the rebus mode is a transformation of imagery into signifiers. Second-level interpretations emerge from the gaze, moved away from an instantaneous recognition of meaning residing in the linkage of text and image, but produced from their juxtaposition and collision. As in Agule's ambigram *Liar*, the rebus mode presents its meaning through the relationship of text to image: we know the man is a liar only because the image and the text converge, but at a distance—their doubling comes specifically from the distinctions between them. The text is the text; while the image is entirely different from this text, yet the meaning can only refer to one specific man whose identification reveals he is a liar. It is a shift from the immanent link of text–image in a mutually reinforcing independent illustration to an excessive meaning *not* present in either image or text alone: rhetoric.

This transformation originates with the graphic aspects of the typeface itself: the appearance of the letters visually. The use of specialized typefaces for different genres of film adds a rhetorical dimension into the comprehension and meaning of the design, one that resides in neither image nor text, but is a function of *how* the text appears—its graphic character reveals "typographic indications of genre,"[3] as noted by Georg Stanitzek—that are in the service of interpretive ends. Once these visual elements begin interacting with the imagistic background, they are the graphic foundation of the rebus mode, described by semiotician Hartmut Stöckl in his article on the semiotics of typefaces:

> Type faces may point to the nature of the document, carry emotional values or indicate the writer's intended audience, and aspects of the layout may serve to reinforce the thematic structure of a given text and facilitate access to its information. Finally, on yet another level of typographic meaning making, the graphic signs of writing can assume pictorial qualities. Thus, letters may form visual shapes which stand for objects from reality, signal states-of-affairs or actions, and illustrate emotions. Materials and techniques of graphic sign making, too, may be made salient in text design and can thus convey something about situation, genre and stylistic intent of a communicative occurrence—this is also a pictorial kind of communication. It is this threefold semiotic nature of typography that provides its communicative flexibility.[4]

Typography on its own communicates through its graphic nature as well as via the lexicon of meanings assigned to language. These additional meanings are reflective of cultural beliefs and biases as much as they are quotational references to earlier designs. The use of stylized ("art") typefaces present this semiotic element of design clearly: the association of slashing letter-forms evocative of Asian calligraphy employed in the various *Charlie Chan* films, or the dominance of slab serif typefaces commonly used to denote westerns with films such as *Rocky Mountain* (1950), *The Searchers* (1956) or *3:10 to Yuma* (1957), and continuing into the present with *The Hateful Eight* (2015). While they do have a rhetorical dimension, it emerges autonomously, a feature of the typeface itself. Thus, the typefaces in these designs are *not* examples of the rebus mode—this association of genre with typeface is *only* a function of the visual aspects of the type itself and does not depend on the images accompanying it. To be a rebus involves a juxtaposition of type *with* imagery that produces a rhetorical excess dependent on absent signifiers evoked rather than shown. Decoding the text–image combination of the rebus mode *requires* cultural lexia established by past knowledge and experience; the simple associations offered by typography *alone* are insufficient to produce the complex plays of intertextuality and immanent encounter in the rebus mode, although the graphic nature of the typeface *can* play a role in these dynamics.

In the title sequence for *Abbott and Costello Meet Frankenstein* (1948) [Figure 4.2], the rebus mode organizes the introduction of the monsters. Animator Walter Lantz's uncredited design uses an elaborate full cel

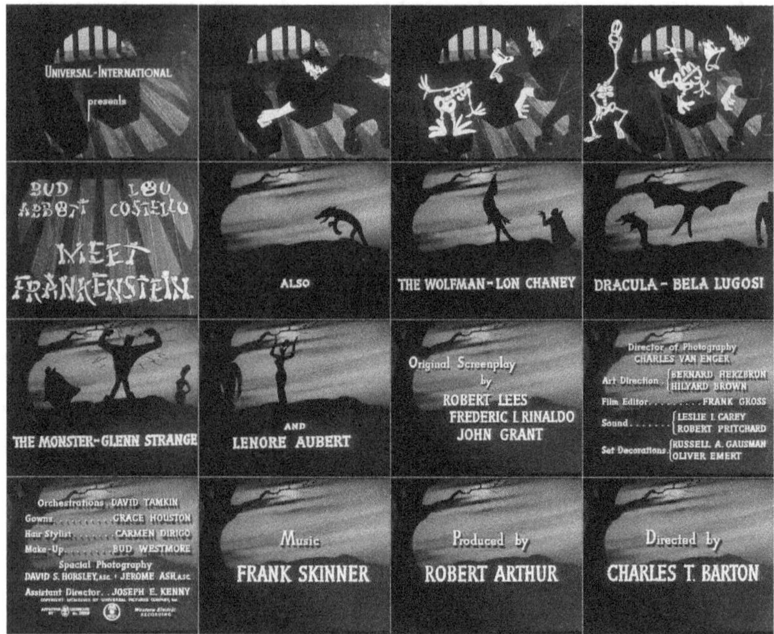

Figure 4.2 All the title cards in *Abbott and Costello Meet Frankenstein* (1948)

animation, unlike his earlier (also uncredited) title designs for Abbott and Costello films such as *Hold That Ghost* (1942), in which the animation is minimal. Running just under 1 minute 30 seconds, it contains thirteen title cards, an appropriate number for a horror-comedy. It is the first film in their series of "Meet the Monsters" spoofs: *Abbott and Costello Meet the Invisible Man*, *Abbott and Costello Meet Dr. Jekyll and Mr. Hyde*, and *Abbott and Costello Meet the Mummy*. Unlike the later films in the series, there are three monsters in *Abbott and Costello Meet Frankenstein*: the werewolf, the vampire, and the eponymous monster. The relations that emerge between the text and animated procession of "villains" in the middle section of this design are an exemplar of the rebus mode, demonstrating its reliance on intertextual knowledge.

The sequence begins with a pair of coffins; the Frankenstein Monster enters and knocks on one, then the other. Abbott and Costello are the scared skeletons "woken up" by its looming presence. The other credits following their collision/transformation into the skeletal title card appear as a procession of silhouettes against a night sky. Each of these outlines performs an emblematic action as they move past, a caption appearing at the bottom of the screen identifying them; this structure is familiar from the calligram mode. All the credits following the "Universal Presents" title card are composed from these same hand-drawn letters that decompose into arrangements of bones. The graphic assembly of the text-names from cartoon-bones-join-image-and-text is an example of the semiotics of typefaces Stöckl describes. It invites the audience to ruminate on past monster movies that showed these same unnatural beings. The interplay between text/bones is a humorous shifting that corresponds to the narrative's own status as a horror-comedy; but without additional visual development on-screen, it will not produce the rebus mode.

The relationship of cartoon character::caption is understandable as a calligram, but with one important difference: the animated cartoon silhouette-outline replaces the photograph for the "monsters" presented in the credits as "THE WOLFMAN—LON CHANEY," "DRACULA—BELA LUGOSI," "THE MONSTER—GLENN STRANGE." These "universal monsters" are known to the audience; their identification via their silhouette's performance is *metonymy*: the substitution of an attribute that replaces the thing itself, here presented by the characteristic performances and appearance of each monster in turn. Their identification via this symbolic characterization renders the presentation rhetorical rather than illustrational, transforming these relations into a rebus, not a calligram.

But this readily identified procession includes a fourth silhouette accompanied by the text "and LENORE AUBERT," whose identity is in doubt: to which of the two female characters appearing in the narrative does this title card refer? The uncertainty of this final identification reveals the uncertainty of the other designations, an ambivalence masked by the apparent certainty of the double identification coupled with the past recognition of actor with a role—Bela Lugosi *is* Dracula, just as Lon Chaney *is* the Wolfman for films of this period; the text::image combination serves to remind the audience of these particular associations of role for each established performer. What is striking about watching this sequence is how immediately clear and unquestioned each title card actually is. Duplicity connects the iconic gesture, itself a determinate signifier, to earlier films with the same actor and role. The iconic performances—the Wolfman's howling, Dracula's cape flowing, Monster's arms outstretched—seem particular, yet their iconic nature renders their connection to a particular actor, specific performance problematic: each iconic silhouette is associated with a *past* film, understanding it requires knowledge of these earlier productions—past cultural knowledge that the current performance specifically invokes. Because there can be no other actor associated with the particular iconic performance; in making this mnemonic link, the divergences and ambiguities of actor/role in the current film disappear via the rhetorical connections of text with these iconic gestures: both the cartoon silhouette and the text are encoded to create a sign *for* that earlier role. It is the connotations that matter in these title cards, not their particulars. By signifying the monster, the animation confirms what the audience reads in the text. Umberto Eco has theorized this intertextual knowledge evoked by the serial structures of Hollywood's productions:

> The form of seriality which in cinema and television is motivated less by the narrative structure than by the nature of the actor himself: the mere presence of John Wayne or Jerry Lewis (when either is not directed by a great director, and even in that case) succeeds in making, always, the same film.[5]

The "star system" Eco describes connects particular actors to specific roles (or types of role) resulting in their performance always being the same—that the actor *becomes* a specific role, and can be no other—this link becomes obvious when we remember that Lon Chaney *is* the Wolfman just as much as Bela Lugosi *is* Dracula. The iconic gesture performed in the title sequence is the minimal referent for evoking these actors' performances: this association of iconic gesture to earlier performance is connotative rather than denotative, depending on audience memory for the connection. But not all these evocations of past films align in *Abbott and Costello Meet Frankenstein*; "The Monster" (Frankenstein) was originally played by Boris Karloff, *not* Glenn Strange. The identification these gestures invoke is immediate for each monster; so direct in fact that when Costello's love interest appears during the first scene, there is no doubt that her engagement with Costello is nefarious even though all of her actions demonstrate serious concern for his wellbeing. The reanimation of these earlier films in the audience's memory—the intertextual dimensions of this design—renders these double captions (role/actor's name) linked to cartoon characters seemingly natural, superficially resembling the calligram mode. However, this title design defers the calligram's immediacy of link between image and text to the audience's memory and past experience with other horror films made at Universal starting in the 1930s—this intertextual transfer between past experience and immanent encounter defines the rebus mode, separating it from the illustrational connections common to the calligram mode that do not depend on intertextual knowledge, instead producing its effect through the *redundancy* of convergent text and image.

"Lenore Aubert" is one of these villains: this information is established by her appearance with them in this procession. However, her villainy is *not* a product of the crediting, but its conventional arrangement on-screen to form a rebus—yet it comes into question because, unlike the three masculine monsters, her identity remains uncertain: there can be only *one* Wolfman, Dracula, or Monster; yet to have several female characters is not unusual—but which one will Aubert play? The uncertainty of this connection between title and narrative action reveals the uncertainty of the other identifications an uncertainty that is literally written into the title sequence itself, which reads, "*Universal presents Abbott and Costello Meet Frankenstein with Lon Chaney—The Wolfman, Dracula—Belo Lugosi, The Monster—Glenn Strange, and Lenore Aubert*" before listing the production credits. If "Frankenstein" refers, as is often the case, to the creation "The Monster," it is strange that the credits should be written this way; however, it is a peculiarity that does not occur to viewers while watching the titles, only when seen as an isolated collection of individual cards.

The presence of "Lenore Aubert" in this procession—along with her gesture, hands on hips, eyes glowing—renders sex and sex appeal (specifically the feminine) as equally supernatural and dangerous as the other *unnatural* terrors of the monsters. Unlike the other silhouette animations, Aubert merely stands and looks at the audience: the danger she poses lies with her self-awareness since she is the only one who has eyes. The "love interest" is monstrous, a danger comparable to the unnatural dangers posed by werewolf, vampire, and golem. This linkage of sex with supernatural monstrosity makes the identification of Aubert's character in the drama that follows immediate, as direct as the recognition of "Lon Chaney" or "Bela Lugosi" by their actions and behaviors.

Multiple, shifting levels of connotation come into the interpretation of a rebus. The shift from graphics to language, and between connotation and denotation, renders these constructs ambiguous but also over determined: title designs engage with past knowledge and experience to produce their meaning as "directly" and "naturally" as any produced through verbal language, but these hermeneutics are unstable, depending on established cultural (intertextual) knowledge, not merely lexical fluency. The "storybook" preamble in Walt Disney's *Snow White and the Seven Dwarfs* (1937) acts to establish the fairy tale nature of the story—that the film is *specifically* a stand-in for a particular, familiar children's story. *Snow White and the Seven Dwarfs* is not a unique or even unusual example of this organization. Similar structures appear in the titles for *Green Light* (Warner, 1937) that turns the pages of a magazine; *Having Wonderful Time* (RKO, 1938) that includes a fan-folded program; *Elephant Boy* (London Film, 1937), based on the book by Rudyard Kipling, uses a book cover and turning pages to establish its connection to the earlier publication. This invocation of the transfer between established knowledge and expectation (the familiar fairy tale) into a new medium, film. Disney's production uses this established, written story identified in the titles through a rhetorical "play" expressed in the preamble—literally showing a "storybook" is facetiously direct; the directness of this presentation makes the rebus mode more apparent through the particular entanglements between the visual design and the narrative content that are in excess to the specifically linguistic statements made by/in the text itself. It is not the design of this text, but its visual presentation that produces the rebus.

The "storybook" is a live action preamble to the animation immediately following the actual title credits. These credits come first, composed from a total of eight title cards (only four title cards credit the animators and staff who made the film). Its structure is a standard example of the figure–ground mode showing type over a static background of amber-colored willemite crystals shot on an animation stand. The "storybook" that follows them begins with what is clearly live action: a decorated book opens and then dissolves into a full-frame view of the page. However, the actual design of the typography and layout of the pages looks like an illuminated manuscript. This opening is organized to draw attention directly to the design of its pages as much as the information this text presents. The visual form matters to its meaning, setting the stage for the fantasy medieval period where the story takes place—a rhetorical excess to the ambiguities of time and place suggested by the text *on* those pages. Understanding this other meaning requires a shifting of focus from the words to their presentation—as "storybook" and as "illuminated pages." It is an identification that happens immediately and without necessarily becoming a conscious part of *how* this presentation impacts its meaning by the audience. The rebus depends on distinct audience recognitions originating with their past experience and knowledge used to interpret what they encounter. This necessary element of established knowledge and expertise hides the rebus in plain sight from those who do not identify the "secret" of its contents.

Abbott and Costello in Jack and the Beanstalk (1955) develops this same dynamic of past knowledge and immanent encounter. This title sequence also assumes the form of a children's picture book, integrating the illuminated manuscript "storybook" into the entire title sequence, the same approach used for *The Adventures of Robin Hood* (Warner, 1938), in which each title card was designed to evoke the pages in a children's storybook. As in the Disney film, this opening for *Abbott and Costello in Jack and the Beanstalk* is composed from live action footage of a storybook literally having its pages turned. The sequence is narrative, a presentation of the children's story in emblematic form: the first card includes the base of the beanstalk, which winds its way up into the sky through each of the following pages until reaching a castle in the sky at the end of the sequence. These rebus examples transform and redirect lower-level meanings towards understandings that are not borne by the text or image, but by the audience's recognitions and deployment of their own prior knowledge and expertise. The simplicity and ease of these connections is facilitated by the familiarity of the devices and narratives invoked by these designs: the audience must recognize the relationship between this sequence and the narrative it portrays, as well as anticipate its transformation in the film that follows, for this peculiar semiotics to come into action; otherwise the title card lapses into lower-level structures of calligram and figure–ground modes.

The Rebus Mode

The appearance of the rebus mode always depends on the past experience and established knowledge of the audience. The rebus mode presents its rhetorical meaning through designs that are easily understood and recognized by the audience without the need for a complex explanation. The audience either recognizes the intertextual elements and is thus able to engage the rebus in its play of reversals and references, or they are not addressed by this form at all; as Eco notes in his discussion of serial form, when confronting the intertextuality of serial works, "what is formed is of no interest; only the way it is formed is interesting."[6] This deployment of established knowledge produces the aesthetic enjoyment of these works, not their specifics, and shows how the interplay of expectation and recognized connection draw from and reward only those audience members who recognize and understand the relationships transformed by the rebus mode.

Italian designer Iginio (aka Eugenio or 'Gigi') Lardani's designs grow in complexity with each new title sequence until he receives his first on-screen credit for the film *The Good, the Bad, and the Ugly* (1966) [Figure 4.3]. His designs for this trilogy start with simple, uncredited graphic animation

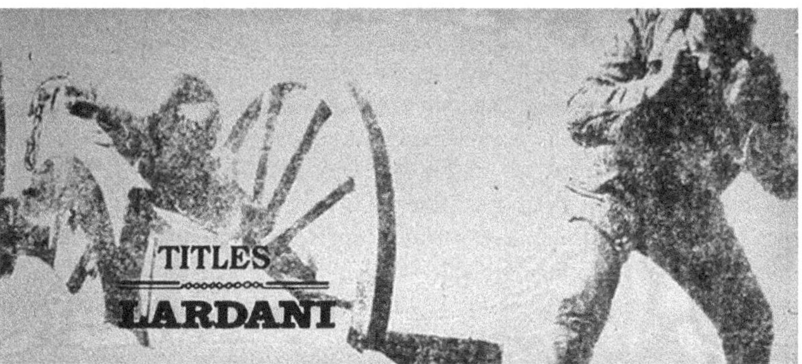

Figure 4.3 A rebus title card showing "Newton's rings" in *The Good, the Bad, and the Ugly* (1966)

in *Fistful of Dollars* (1964), progressing to animated typography 'mapped' to imitate cloud shadows rolling across an extreme long shot of landscape in *For A Few Dollars More* (1965) until he received on-screen credit in *The Good, the Bad, and the Ugly*. This third title sequence contains three different kinds of material—animation, composited masks/text, and hold frames tinted with a colored filter—all created by precise, careful work on an optical printer: the static background shots are made from 'holds' on live action imagery from the film itself that have been optically printed with a film stock that would accentuate their grainy texture, such as HiCon. These "posterized" hold frames were rephotographed again with a colored filter to tint the shot, and composited with other HiCon masks made by filming a brush painting, smoke swirling, or something granular being poured to create the distinctive (and dramatic) white transitions that resolve into the typography itself. This third title design includes a singular rebus that addresses only a small portion of the audience for the film: for the unaware viewer, this design simply presents a figure–ground mode title where his credit is superimposed over a photograph of a canon.

However, for a viewer who understands the technical process of optical printing commonly used in creating title sequences, there is an entirely different meaning presented by the rebus mode: an "error" specific to optical printing caused by improper loading of the footage and mask being composited—*Newton's rings*—appears in his title card alongside the text stating "TITLES | LARDANI." It is a technical mistake unique in this design to Lardani's own credit. Recognizing this specific 'error' in the card stating "TITLES LARDANI" depends on technical knowledge of the optical printing process. Its presence in the title sequence is especially striking because the rest of the sequence unfolds as a virtuosic execution of optical printing to create multiple, complex composites, a dramatic aesthetic and technical expansion over his earlier title sequences; given the technical perfection in the rest of the sequence, it is not just a "beginner's mistake," but implies a *conscious* choice to include this compositing error in the design.

Recognizing the rebus mode in this title card also requires acknowledging the differences between *his* on-screen credit and the *other* credits in the rest of the title sequence: his title card is shorter in duration, running just under 3 seconds, while other titles are 5+ seconds long; the text is in black rather than created by a white mask; it is not composed to use the "type hole"—that portion of the image typically left empty for typography—rendering it difficult to read his credit due to a lack of contrast between the type and the image behind it; the image chosen for this card has a distinctly comical character in a dramatic, even dour, montage of actors and civil war imagery; it contains an error, when no other shot in the sequence has *any* apparent 'error.' These features distinguish Lardani's credit from the rest of the sequence in a very dramatic way—unlike the other titles which are immediately obvious *as* credits, it is possible to miss his credit entirely, a strange distinction to choose given his role and, according[7] to his son, complete freedom in creating the design. It is almost as if his title card is hidden in plain sight [Figure 4.4].

This 'glitched' card is also the *only* comical image in a title sequence otherwise composed from serious, dramatic materials. Shots of the three leads with serious expressions, and images evoking the US Civil War are hardly imagery capable of provoking laughter, yet Tuco (who is the "Ugly" from the film's title) *is* a comic figure in the background image chosen for Lardani's credit: he is firing a canon with fingers in his ears and eyes

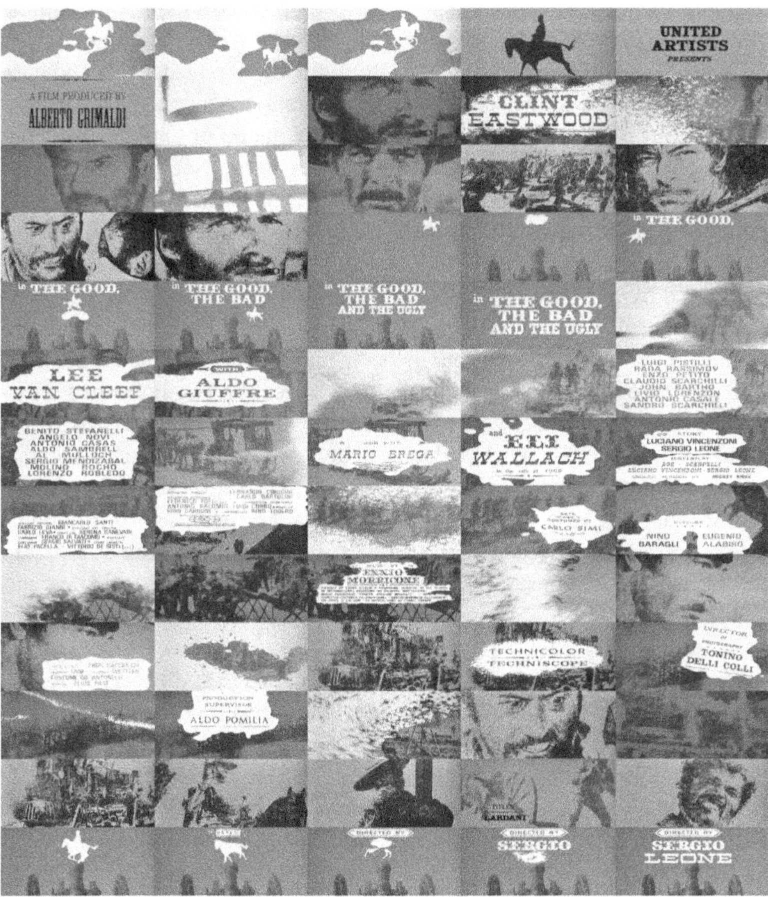

Figure 4.4 All the title cards in *The Good, the Bad, and the Ugly* (1966)

clenched shut, suggesting a denial of what he can see and hear. The choice of this picture for this specific title card is suggestive, inviting an allegorical interpretation. Tuco's appearance here may be an allegorical stand-in for Lardani himself, the *Newton's rings* (error) an indication of what can happen when the designer doesn't watch what he's doing—the error thus humorously acknowledging the precision and attention to detail required in compositing with an optical printer.

This comic metaphor of the inattentive designer is doubled by interpreting Tuco as a stand-in for Lardani, not just as a statement about how the title designer must pay attention to his craft or it will go wrong, but also specifically because this is Lardani's *own* credit—the announcement that Lardani *is* figuratively and literally responsible for the mistake. *He* is the *designer* of these titles. It is a joke *only* comprehensible (even recognizable) by an audience that recognizes the *Newton's rings* and understands what they are—an error in the optical printing; this knowledgeable audience specifically includes title sequence designers rather than the general public.

The rebus mode offers an allegorical interpretation of Lardani's first on-screen credit. Because it is specifically a specialized, *technical* mistake, its recognition will be severely limited to his peers—suggesting they are the ones being addressed by it. This card can thus be understood as an "in joke" for them: Lardani seeks to join this elite group "with a bang"—a reading reinforced by the location of his credit at the base of the canon, where its fuse is located. Canons reappear as animation throughout this design performing a very specific function. In the beginning of the sequence, the main title was introduced by firing a canon three times at a tiny horseman crossing the screen, with the words "The Good," followed by "The Bad," and finally "And the Ugly," each replacing a tiny cowboy and his horse; the final credit, announcing "directed by SERGIO LEONE" follows a similar format of the canon firing to make the words appear. The inclusion of the glitch (*Newton's rings*) in Lardani's own title card then simply becomes a part of his signature, a demonstration of mastery over both the technical apparatus and the design process through his inclusion of what would otherwise be a basic technical mistake.

Provided audiences have the necessary knowledge and expertise to recognize and "unravel" the rebus, they navigate between first-level and second-level easily, without the need for a conscious choice as the sequence develops. Distinctions between first-level and second-level modes arise from shifts from apparently fixed relationships in the first-level to the ambiguities of allegory in which opposed engagements of reading::seeing interact to produce a new, rhetorical meaning. Marking the distinction between these modes—the interplay between telling::showing, reading::seeing, and text::image—enables the recognition of the second-level relationships active in the rebus mode. These shifting meanings reflect the fluidity of interpretation as title sequences develop on-screen, engagements that are apparent any time text and image appear together in a motion picture.

Ambivalence is central to rhetoric, an elliptical combination that challenges established lexical meaning. The redirection from depiction towards its metonymic potentials realizes this forced juxtaposition via indirect connections between a text::image. A title card such as "screenplay by Horton Foote," superimposed over a photograph of a crayon in Steven Frankfurt's design for *To Kill a Mockingbird* (1962), is typical of the simple form of the rebus mode [Figure 4.5]. In discovering the connection, the audience must recognize a sequence of links and ellipses between a crayon used by children to draw and scrawl words and the structured, carefully organized process of writing a screenplay; that it is the same crayon used to "reveal" the film title is not a coincidence. However, the text superimposed on this image does *not* create a calligram. The crayon does not illustrate "screenplay by Horton Foote" in the way that an actor illustrates their name—the text "Liam Neeson" in *Unknown* reiterates the background image. Yet there *is* an apparent link in *To Kill a Mockingbird*: these cards employ the familiar logic of metonymy—this crayon *does* stand for the act of adapting the screenplay from the novel. It is a strictly linguistic meaning translated into visual form, deferring their connection until the audience acknowledges the relationship of text and associated photograph. These erratic features of language are specifically discontinuous, requiring imaginative leaps to join

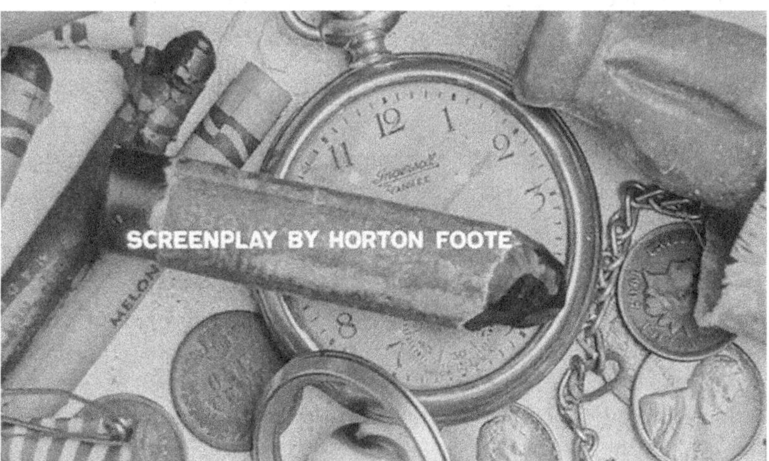

Figure 4.5 A rebus stating, "screenplay by Horton Foote," from *To Kill a Mockingbird* (1962)

them; the foundation for this type of association is the rebus (like the calligram, it is familiar from childhood), a puzzle where words and concepts are partially replaced by imagery whose decipherment produces a new meaning distinct from its component. It is a logic of synthesis arising from a conjunction of elements, each specifically distinct from another.

The rhetoric engaged by this process is incompatible with first-level illustrative links between telling::showing—the picture is never an illustration of the statement made by the text. Instead of one dominating the other, text and image have equal weight in their interpretation; the precarity of their balance animates their meaning, forcing a resolution where they fuse as the rebus. The metaphor rendered visual depends on perceived connections via metonymies between image and text. Their conceptual recognition is not apparent in these relations precisely in how this disjunctive connection directs attention away from the illustrative. Until the linkage is made between image and text—a sudden burst of comprehension produced by deciphering them—the rebus remains unrecognized, invisible, masquerading as the figure–ground mode.

In the simple form, the connections of *crayon–writing* are relatively direct links whose metonymic functions easily emerge from how the image stands in for the activity identified by the text. The screenplay may not have been written in crayon, but it could be; in each case there is an apparent relationship between the thing depicted and the activity described. In this recognition of how the image implies what the text names, the two enter into a mutual dialogue about the nature of these actions and their meaningful re-presentation on-screen. The categorical classifications of text and image remain unchallenged in themselves in the simple form: text remains linguistic, while image remains graphic—their combination in the rebus mode does not require a violation of these relations for its meanings to emerge.

However, these transformations of indirect connections of image to text via rhetorical association using metonymy—the crayon evoking action of writing itself—changes the fixed, controlled relationship of telling::seeing into a mobilization of past knowledge and experience that unravel the rebus's associative connections. Thus, the same affirmation of a dominant order through visualized knowledge Foucault recognizes as characteristic of calligrams (and title sequences generally) is especially evident in the rebus, but changed into an explicit assertion of that order. Forcing a consideration of an allegorical meaning, independent of the images/texts alone, is a deflection of photography's representational status, a transfiguration of "connotation" to become "denotation" as Foucault notes about the changed meanings produced by the rebus:

> The similar develops in series that have neither beginning nor end, that can be followed in one direction as easily as in another, that obey

> no hierarchy, but propagate themselves from small differences among small differences. Resemblance serves representation, which rules over it; similitude serves repetition, which ranges across it.[8]

The rebus mode renders the image as denotation; Foucault's distinction of semblance and resemblance describes the movement from mimetic depiction into the realm of semiotics where images become text in the shift between reading::seeing. Abandoning immanent recognition for a generalized meaning, necessarily rhetorical, defines the rebus. The crayon comes to resemble the associated activity—writing—as ciphers functioning not by their representation specificity (resemblance) but thorough abstraction as general signs; this rhetorical deflection is characteristic of the rebus. The similarity between depiction and concept invoked through the text resolves the rebus as a visualized metaphor whose meaning comes from a forced similarity between ambivalent image and lexical meaning. Foucault's "similitude" is this condition of language, of terms whose meanings emerge from their contextual transformation; it produces what he identifies as rhetoric:

> It uses the possibility of repeating the same thing in different words and profits from the extra richness of language that allows us to say different things with a single word. The essence of rhetoric is in allegory.[9]

Where a calligram's joining of text to image produces a doubling or reinforcing of the same meaning, the rebus mode creates a *new* meaning independent of what the image shows. The rebus transforms depiction (which always aspires to be what it shows) into a sign whose meaning is *other* than the depiction. Rhetoric is not just a series of terms arranged, but their deflection and transformation via juxtaposition in series, one term altering the meaning of the next—these changes happen fluently for the audience—as when "lightning" modifies and is transformed by "bug" (nobody confuses the meaning of "lightning" and "lightning bug"). The rebus resolves image not as depiction, but as a sign (i.e., connotation).

Transforming *vision* into *reading* the rhetorical shift around crayon/writing in Frankfurt's design allegorically allows these references to move beyond the immediate and superficial representation of writing by this crayon to become at the same moment also a statement about the nature and source of that writing. The choice of *this* crayon, worn and thick—which appears in use elsewhere in the title sequence rubbing over type to reveal the film's title, drawing a bird—is necessary to firmly identify the writing as a child's story; the narrative is from a child's perspective. The entire sequence is implicated in this single title card. Thus the association of crayon with "screenplay by Horton Foote" suggests the point of view employed in the film, beyond just the metonymic linkage of writing with an implement. The apparent challenge to vision as knowledge is a chimera since selection of this *particular* image (photography is always specific) foreshadows and anticipates the drama. These relations between title cards and story are common for title sequences of this type—the encapsulation of the film that follows within the opening is often a metanarrative of the film that follows rendered as a puzzle (rebus) whose decipherment is held in suspension because its lexicon is the drama itself: the story whose events unfold *after* the title sequence is over. Nevertheless, decoding this rebus happens immediately, a spontaneous recognition of the relationship and its meaning the audience performs fluently. The differences between reading::seeing may be fundamental, but they are also familiar and readily navigated.

Allegory transforms representation into metaphor, in the process shifting the significance of what is seen so its material form serves interpretative ends; instead of being, it signifies. The particularities of the image matter, but only in so far as they engage this new function, as a rebus born in a complication of the typical relations between text::image. It is a re-reading of the image as language that characterizes a simple variant of the rebus. In denying the representational mimesis of photography, the dominance of vision as a giving-level affirms the established hierarchies of thought and interpretation. These recognitions and shift happen readily and fluidly, this process being instantaneous since it is the same sequence of shifts between image and language commonly employed in reading text itself.

Text as Graphic Transition

The opposition of reading::seeing becomes especially apparent in the organization of the rebus employed for Pablo Ferro's opening sequence in *Bullitt* (1968) [Figure 4.6]. The design of this entire sequence, where the opening montage has been replaced by a complex series of masks and repeating shots fusing the opening montage with animated typography via compositing to present the on-screen credits (the title cards), is designed as a rebus, an appropriate organization for a crime drama. What the narrative chronicles is the discovery of reasons—motives—for this opening montage that is simultaneously the title sequence. This fact defines the mystery genre itself, and is what unifies all detective stories: whether they are concerned with the meandering investigation of a private investigator or following the police as they make their inquiries, they are concerned with piercing the veil of surface illusions—the lies, deceit, and misinformation criminals use to hide their crimes.

Ferro's title sequence is set in syncopation to the jazz it accompanies: the pace and timing of the sequence matches the music. As 'Steve McQueen'

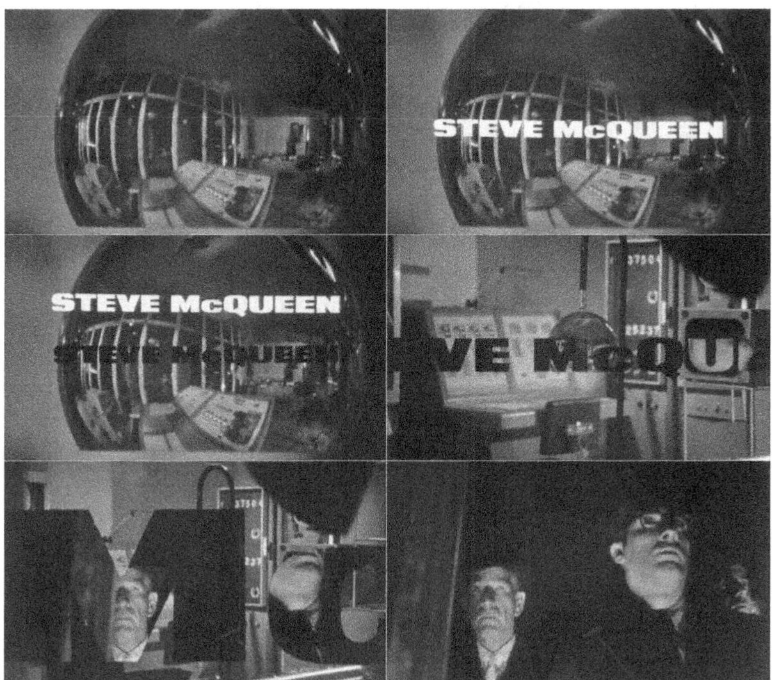

Figure 4.6 Composite made with text masks in *Bullitt* (1968)

fades up in white against a tracking shot of a deserted office at night, the name slides vertically up the screen, leaving behind a "type hole" (the shape of the name) that grows larger, revealing a different tracking shot in motion inside/ behind it. This organization remains constant through most of these titles, providing the transitions between shots in place of a simple cut. The rebus develops from how the typography introduces each of the principle actors: their name comes on-screen, then when it exits, its 'hole' provides the "cut" to the next shot: the optically printed kinetic typography in white leaves a "window" into a second image. This rebus is *literally* the process of discovery dramatized by this opening sequence. In place of editing, this optically printed composite suggests movement *into* or *beneath* these images: while the white typography slides off screen, the holes behind it grow larger, expanding, and in the process, revealing a new shot. The text becomes a graphic image—a rebus—the transition between shots, replacing traditional editing.

The opening images repeat—in full color and again in a red-tinted black-and-white—emphasizing the dualities and duplicities associated with crime.

This duplicity is at the same time also the duplicity of reading::seeing contained by the rebus itself, a pairing that the audience recognizes, forcing their engagement to constantly shift modes. Unlike many detective stories where the audience can engage with the facts and attempt to deduce who is guilty, in *Bullitt*, this title sequence/opening is both a crime scene and a series of clues. The question invoked by this narrative is not *who did it*, but *why?* and answering this question is the real focus of the film's plot and mystery. These titles are thus not simply an independent reflection of/on the film, but an integral part of the story: the final shot of this sequence reveals that the man in the office was under (literal) attack by his brother—who also happens to be his business partner; the office under assault is their shared office. *Why did this sequence of events happen?* is the question explicitly raised by the concluding shot of the title sequence; it is essential to the dramatic narrative, posing the central mystery itself, whose answer drives the events of the plot.

Yet while the mise-en-scene of these opening shots is essential to the detective story that follows, its particular transformation through the optically printed title sequence is not. The rebus develops around paranoia and mistrust of appearances. Even though it is possible that the repetition of shots in full color and as tinted black-and-white was used to increase the duration of these shots so there would be enough footage for all the contractually required titles (a more traditional montage sequence would have an entirely different timing and character without Ferro's optical transitions), this title design is clearly an integral part of how the narrative develops the mystery posed by this particular opening, whether or not this precise composition of titles and transitions was the "originally" planned opening sequence for the film as a whole. The rebus replaces montage with this graphic movement *into*, transforming the meaning of the sequence. To answer the questions posed by the dramatic events in the opening sequence requires a consideration of the doublings that appear throughout it. This analysis leads to considerations of the visual relationships in excess to their verbal content, or the montage they reshape.

Ferro's use of optically printed 'windows' that act as the typography is not unique to *Bullitt*. Michelangelo Antonioni's film *Blow Up* (1966), released three years earlier, offers an alternative execution of this same design approach: as with *Bullitt*, *Blow Up* employs optically printed titles that composite two different shots together to produce a "window" into a second shot behind (beneath?) the first [Figure 4.7]. However, unlike *Bullitt*, this typography remains in place, showing a series of different shots that cut normally within the lettering superimposed over the green lawn of a park. While this shot of a lawn is a continuous long take, the typography appears and disappears, the image in each title card contains a different shot

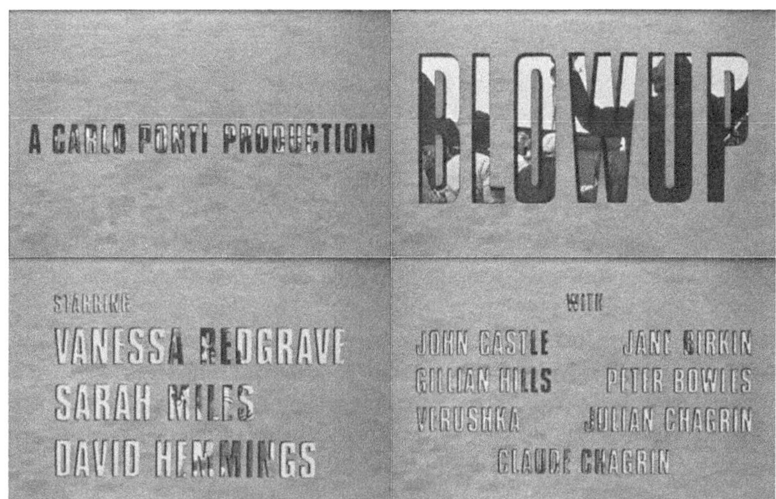

Figure 4.7 Composites made with text masks in *Blow Up* (1966)

of women (?) in Mod clothing, dancing. The edits are 'held' within (as) the contents of the text as the shots change with each new title card, providing a strong contrast to the nearly static image of green grass. This use of a long take as the 'background' for a title sequence is typical for feature films starting in the 1920s, as is the use of optical printing to insert the typography. The dynamic set-up between duality of the "long-take/montage" contained by the individual layers of image and the fragmentation imposed by the graphic transitions renders the particularity of the text thus employed irrelevant: *whose* credits are immaterial, it is the motion into, through, and under that these transitions produce that is important. The titles to *Blow Up* are a rebus that implies a second reality beneath the visible one of the park, yet this title/sequence does not develop this implication beyond simply posing it. In contrast to the titles for *Blow Up*, *Bullitt* does develop this implication, moving into narrative exposition—the sequence shows a crime happening—allowing the doubling of shots to become part of the 'performance' given by the actors.

The replacement of standard cutting (montage) by this optical compositing of shots produces a revelational affect: the sense in watching the sequence, and the implication presented by this construction, is that of a search *within* the space of this vacant, rather mundane, office. Each transition suggests movement forward ('going deeper'). The implied shift is clearly spatial—the emergence of a 'new' space behind/within the shot. It reveals something about what appears on-screen. What is 'discovered' in this process as the titles appear one by one is anticipatory: the office initially appears in the convex reflection of a lamp, countered by a rogues' gallery of rough-looking men standing in the dark, their faces lit from below, seen en mass via a tracking shot. The images reveal these men as they assault this office, breaking the plate glass windows and rushing in, guns blazing—an attack on a single individual who escapes by using a smoke grenade. Violence, smoke and mirrors, misdirection—*what is happening?*—these are the elements of that are expected of a mystery story. Answering the questions posed by this 3.5-minute opening title/sequence organizes the plot for the rest of the film. However, the organization of these shots amplifies the narrative significance and obliquely comments on it; these shifts between paratext and interpretation are precisely typical of the rebus mode.

The rebus mode's commentary emerges from both masking titles and camera work in the shots—a play of counterpoint between title cards (text), kinetic typography (masks), and the live action photography (backgrounds). The sequence initially proceeds in a stable, recognizable fashion, even if it is disorienting spatially: the first image is an aerial tracking shot of Chicago at night, accompanied by the Warner Brothers logo; this initial shot ends with darkness that is replaced by a cut to a close-up of a mirrored ball lamp showing an anamorphic reflection, distorted and elongated, of a typical mid-century Modern office: grey metal desks, letter boxes, typewriters, and chairs. As the shot zooms out, Steve McQueen's name fades up in the center of the frame, then moves vertically out of shot, allowing the expanding type to reveal the rogues' gallery in red-tinted black-and-white. The initial non-specific disorientation continues as details of this space resolve into an inside::outside opposition—society versus rogues. The main title card stating "in Bullitt" | "a Solar Production" fades up and the optical transition repeats, showing a tracking shot past the office windows, looking in; initially in full color, the shift produced by the title card "Robert Vaughn" changes this view for an identical shot, but repeating the pan and in the same tinted black-and-white as before. When the mask saying "Jacqueline Bissett" fills the screen, revealing a full-color version of the rogues, the optically printed sequence ends, and it cuts to a long take panning around the office in deep focus, collapsing the space on-screen into a confusing shallow space: adding machines and desktop clutter overlap, details near and far merge kaleidoscopically. It is a pan that suggests a search, looking *for* someone or something, but not finding it.

The doubled shots that shift between full color and tinted black-and-white are significant for the meaning of this sequence; it is a purely visual duplication that becomes a signifier through its reiteration of movement *into* the space. While the narrative dimension of this montage is simple—a group of men break into an office at night—the doubling of shots alters the significance of this action: it becomes a revelation of a much darker, sinister side to what is otherwise an unexceptional office space. The alternation of full-colored/tinted shots presents this specific meaning: that the world of crime is a darker, "bloodier" (red) version of the familiar world. That it is not only outside our familiar spaces (the rogues' gallery) but lies just below the surface of our familiar interiors—this meaning appears through the shift introduced by the repetition of the tracking shot: in color for Robert Vaughn and switching to a tinted repeat of that same shot mid-way across the space for Jacqueline Bissett. We see only a glimpse of the rogues in full color before cutting back to the full-color searching pan of the office.

The first view of this office space [Figure 4.6] anticipates this duplicity: it initially appears as a highly distorted reflection in the curved mirrored surface of a globular desk lamp, giving a panoramic view of the entire office space—but this wide-angle view also suggests the distorted spaces of security mirrors. The shot following it is the initial, tinted view of the rogues' gallery—a view that repeats in color as the scene that momentarily lies beneath Jacqueline Bissett's name. What are these men looking at? They stand, arrayed in a black space, frontally lit, clearly peering *at* something: point-of-view is unstable in these titles, shifting between inside looking out and outside looking in, but of particular importance is the collision between the full-color and tinted shots that circle back between color and tinted, inside and outside, criminals and office space. That these men are on the other side of the glass, about to begin an assault on a lone man inside the office, becomes obvious as the sequence develops, but even this relationship is ambiguous. While the searching gaze and tracking shot through the windows can be linked to the criminals' gazing in, what about the other images in the sequence? The views afforded of the smoke grenade, the lone man's flight from the office, and his escape through the parking garage cannot easily be linked to any particular gaze. But even those shots that do imply a connection to particular characters—the tracking shot for example—become problematic because they are doubled: what does the shifting of color/tinting mean for this supposed point of view? These questions undermine the simple assignment of shot-to-character's sight, directly contributing to the ambiguities of the structure that make these first opening shots disorienting.

This ungrounding of what would otherwise be a very stable and coherent variation on the standard shot/reverse shot montage is significant for what this sequence suggests about crime: its universality—that it is *not* something lurking in the dark just outside our windows, but is really just beneath the surface, always present, already in progress—we just aren't aware it's there, is happening, until it bursts into view. This understanding of crime and criminality blurs the boundary between the more traditional Hollywood film depiction of "white hat vs. black hat" where 'good' and 'evil' are nominally separate, discrete entities that never come into contact. The moral ambiguity of crime just under the surface manifests through how the rebus structures the montage—the movement between color and tinted versions of the same images, their repetition, the looping organization of these first composited transitions: the first cut once these titles have begun follows Jacqueline Bissett's name, moving from a full-color close-up of the rogues to another full-color close-up of a typewriter on a desk inside the office as the searching pan around the office resumes/continues.

The rebus doubles these opening shot-transitions, producing confusion, forcing the viewer to search the images shown, in effect casting the audience in the role of detective/criminal as the opening plays out on-screen. The dominant character in this opening sequence is not human—it is the office itself, that space under observation. However, the gaze represented through the pan around that office has a specific locus: the rogues outside the windows, looking in—a reversal of the normal relationship of reading::seeing. Vision dominates this sequence, suppressing the reading required for the credits in favor of their role as graphic elements. The act of searching, shown by the pan and its analogous role (the detective) forced on the audience by the disorientation of this opening, is at the same time specifically connected to this group of unknown men looking in and —has a "criminal intent" that spectacularly emerges. That these men outside/looking in are criminals is not in doubt: their presentation through the initial tinted tracking shot, the low frontal lighting, their inky black background, and their particular faces all communicate the archetypal Hollywood image of the criminal henchman; that they are members of the mafia is not in doubt from the first time they appear on-screen. Ambivalence is the defining characteristic of the rebus, dominating the interpretation of this title/preamble. The connection of criminal to detective—produced by the connection of the searching gaze to these men—reinforces the confusion of 'good' and 'evil' (the criminal and the law-abiding citizen) that emerges from the visual doubling of these opening shots. Their linkage in this title sequence (even equivalence) poses a moral ambiguity about them that extends into the events of the main narrative; in this regard, the titles encapsulate the unsettling and paranoid dimensions of this detective story in which the villains are as likely to be the police as not. However, unlike later films such as *The French Connection* (1971) or *McQ* (1973), the internal corruption of the police department[10] is incidental to the real focus of the narrative: the ambiguity inherent in politics and the social decay that results from the pursuit of personal political ambitions. The crime that appears in this opening sequence is merely the catalytic pretext for the broader consideration of these issues within the main narrative plot. While none of these dimensions are directly apparent in this title/montage, they are suggested by the specific *space* of the events shown: an apparently ordinary office of the type that might be seen anywhere in the United States in the 1950s and 1960s.

This rebus develops the moral ambiguity particular to detective stories. It organizes the troubling dimensions of both story and title sequence, an ambiguity that was of great concern in the late 1960s; *Bullitt* was released in 1968, the same year that writer W.H. Auden published his discussion of detective stories:

> I suspect that the typical reader of detective stories is, like myself, a person who suffers from a sense of sin. From the point of view of ethics, desires and acts are good and bad, and I must choose the good and reject the bad, but the *I* which makes this choice is ethically neutral; it only becomes good or bad in its choice. To have a sense of sin means to feel guilty at there being an ethical choice to make, a guilt which however 'good' I may become, remains unchanged.[11]

The ambiguity that troubles Auden is the uncertainty made literally apparent in the duplicity of this opening sequence—a rebus where the significance of what happens becomes a revelation of society at large: revealed not just through the repeating shots, but through the coincidence of gazes—the criminals and the audience both engage in the act of detection (become detectives). This opening positions the audience in the same uncertain space and role as the criminals. The audience's complicity with those criminals becomes a feature of *how* the space of this generic office appears; it is also an innate part of the relations set up by the modal shifts of reading::seeing that inform the title/sequence. What initially appears to be a neutral gaze—the unseen camera—reveals itself as the partisan view of the criminal/audience/detective looking into this space, searching . . . but for what, exactly? As Foucault has noted, the gaze serves to render its subject comprehensible, orderly; the rebus mode makes this domination a contingency, apparent to the audience for how it emerges ambivalently from the shifts between reading title cards and seeing (through) the masking-transitions. The difference between the criminals' search and the audience's lies with exactly this difference: the criminals' search is targeted, precise, while the audience's, in contrast, is not—where the audience is looking for meaning, the criminals seek only confirmation of what they already know. Their certainty is at one and the same time a demonstration of their having already resolved the ethical problem posed by Auden—they have chosen 'bad' instead of 'good.' For the audience watching this sequence develop, that the criminals' choice has been made is guaranteed by their appearance and location—outside, looking in—as much as by their actions: they break the windows and enter the office, guns blazing, firing blindly into this well-lit space. The duality of criminals outside (in darkness) and interior office (brightly lit) is countered by the duality of shots that transform the bright interior into an equally darkened space—a space that before and during their assault is itself transformed into a confusing labyrinth of reflections and smoke. The moral ambiguity is not just a feature of the title's doubling of shots, it is also part of their initial framing, reflecting this uncertainty at all levels of this title/sequences' construction.

The rebus mode's instability gives these titles their initial sense of the uncanny: that this office space is not what it appears to be, transformed into a crime scene about to happen. But while the sequence begins with this displacement and doubling, as it progresses, these uncertainties are resolved in clear ways: the criminals are outside, breaking in; the office is not as deserted and unaware of their actions as it initially seemed. The alignment of these actions with the emergent understanding of events corresponds to the unraveled rebus. The discovery of meaning is at the same time a recognition of dramatic roles within this title design. That the criminals run for cover when the lights come on (their awkwardness and speed reminiscent of cockroaches running when the kitchen light goes on) reinforces their marginal position and that their actions are illicit. The certainty of the man lying in wait inside, the deliberate presentation of his pulling the pin from a smoke grenade, and subsequent escape from the criminals makes his actions as the 'defender' a signifier of preparedness against the coming onslaught of the rogues' gallery looking in. Even as the opening shots suggest danger, and through their repetition implicate this office space in crime, the singularity of the second half of the titles—there are no more doubled shots—coupled with the actions taken to evade, defend, and escape the criminals serve as a consolation: while crime does invade the safety of the mundane office, it is basically foreign and the 'residents' of that office are not unaware of the pressing danger. The affect this sequence offers is thus one where the initial threats and moral ambiguity—capable of provoking panic—is swiftly countered as the narrative develops. The shift from moral ambiguity and uncertainty about crime guilt (resolved by events of the main narrative focused on the identification of the true criminals, their unmasking, and capture/punishment) finds itself repeated in miniature as the rebus presented by the title/sequence itself.

Text as Image

In the simple variant, the *text* of the title remains stable, performing its typical functions as language—the visual aspects of the words play a role in the significance of their meaning only in terms of their legibility (capacity to be recognized as letter-forms); however, the rebus also has a complex variant, emergent not from shifts in the role of the image, but from the design and presentation of the text—its style and dress—the imagistic character of language introducing meanings not contained by the text itself. Where the simple form is a rhetorical transformation of imagery, in the complex form it depends on a rhetoric around the *form* of the type and its *arrangement* on-screen. Both variants retain the same formal relationship between text and image. However, in a complex rebus, the type also becomes an *additional* "image" ignored in the other modes.

Pablo Ferro's first credited design, for *Dr. Strangelove, or how I learned to stop worrying and love the bomb* (1964), employs his signature irregular lines and wobbly letters to form asymmetrical compositions where the outlines of words fill the screen, but due to their narrowness, the background remains visible [Figure 4.8]. This sequence is composed from two distinct sections: first, a voice-over narrative preamble accompanying aerial footage of cloud-shrouded mountains running 40 seconds; then the title sequence itself, running approximately 110 seconds and containing eighteen title cards that either fade-in-and-out, or dissolve one into the next, overlaid onto only eight background images. The narrative's satire of the Cold War is reflected by the design of the lettering used *for* the title cards, as well as in the sexual innuendo apparent in his editing of stock footage of B-52 bombers refueling (mating) midair to an instrumental rendition of Laurie Johnson's "Try a little tenderness." In contrast to other title sequences of the 1950s and early

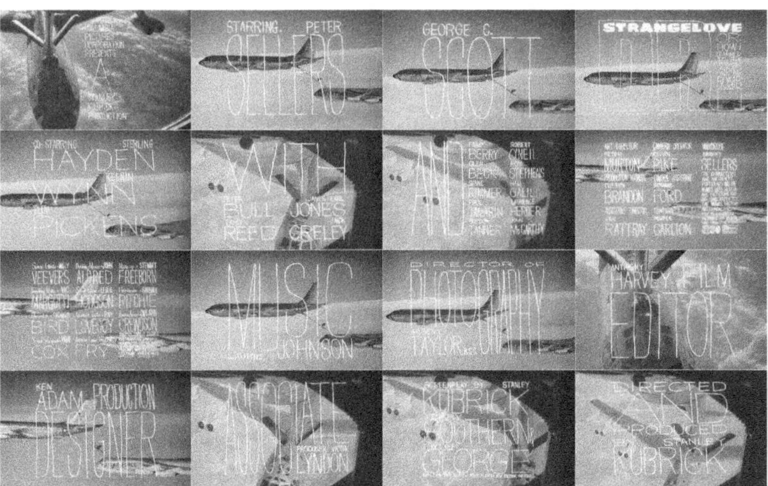

Figure 4.8 All the title cards in *Dr. Strangelove, or how I learned to stop worrying and love the bomb* (1964)

1960s, the title cards for *Dr. Strangelove* are clearly hand-drawn. There are only three distinct views of B-52s used as backgrounds for superimposed type: two from inside the refueling plane, looking down onto the bomber, and one from the side showing the fuel line linking the two aircraft; it opens with a view up from below at the refueling line (resembling a large metal phallus). Shots seem to repeat, joined by a change of image—back inside the refueling plane—enabling a longer sequence than the quantity of footage might otherwise allow. Repetition of background shots renders them consistently recognizable even when obscured by a large quantity of text.

The critical meaning offered by the rebus mode in this design is contextually determined by its subversive relationship to then-dominant modernist conceptions of order expressed through typography and design. The oscillation between reading::seeing establishes the complex variant as a repudiation of demands for an untheorized legibility common to modernist design noted by Jan-Christopher Horak in his discussion of Saul Bass.[12] The design of each title card in Ferro's first title sequence challenges this assumption through the identification of the letter-forms as both image *and* text: the graphic character of these title cards as well as their composition on-screen draws attention to them *as* visual forms in addition to their meaning-bearing function *as* text; it is a design that denies language to assert the words-as-image.

The reversion of letters to graphics is an opening of language onto other types of meaning not explicitly contained by the lexia itself—a formal rhetoric of shape and design inflects the over-determined meaning of the text as such—a rupture of these fundamental conceptions of typography as primarily a vehicle for reading. In a rare theoretical discussion of this approach, graphic designer Douglas C. McMurtrie identifies this "modern approach" in 1929 with a denial of the graphic nature of both the typography and its composition-arrangement:

> "Pretty" layouts on the one hand, and exceedingly bizarre arrangements on the other are to be frowned upon as diverting attention from the message itself to the physical form of its typography, which is always to be considered not as an end in itself, but only as a means to the end that the message can be read. For like reasons, ornamentation in the usual sense is excluded from the Modern typography. The only purpose of ornament is to make the layout an attractive picture, which is not a proper aim, as the sole object should be to get the printed story comprehended by the reader. Anything standing in the way of this objective must be sacrificed.[13]

His clearly stated bias against the complexities of the rebus generally may be the reason for its relative historical rarity; the complexity of the rebus mode is an existential challenge to any conception of typography focused on creating and asserting a "transparent meaning." This reversal is definitional for the complex rebus: it renders language into something that must be *seen* rather than *read*, undoing the semiotic functions of language to give primacy to the visuality of language submerged in the act of reading. McMurtrie's denial of meanings presented through the design and composition correspond precisely to an affirmation of Foucault's systems of control and order; the title sequence itself acts as an affirmation of these systems: the names appear in a certain order, at certain sizes agreed upon governed by traditions and often formally written into the contracts. This dominant system of importance and its hierarchical construction of roles are parodied by the excessively mismatched and out-of-scale credits in Ferro's design. Compositions of individual title cards parody the title sequence's own self-importance: the credit—*the name*—is often significantly smaller than the role performed. Other, disproportionately large parts of these text compositions have a self-aggrandizing character that contrasts with their actual contents: the giant "AND" accompanied by a list of ten names, or the equally outsized "DESIGNER" paired with a small "KEN ADAM." The "designer title" introduced by Saul Bass in 1954 with *Carmen Jones* and visibly "signed" with his on-screen credit makes the prestige and egotism of having a spot in title sequence a feature of title design itself—precisely the concern with dominance and the projection of power that the *Dr. Strangelove* title sequence satirizes as a futile attempt at demonstrating virility: the "MAIN TITLES BY PABLO FERRO" is wedged in-between much larger names, making his credit *literally* an afterthought, apparently added at the last minute (as Ferro himself has repeatedly claimed). This critique emerges through the mismatched scale of names/roles in the screen-filling compositions of text. The same aspirational, dominant masculinity is reiterated throughout the narrative as well—the eponymous Doctor's "ten women to each man" required for the survival of the human race being the most self-evident example.

The structural relationships between typography, graphics, and live action in *Dr. Strangelove* are not merely a function of the hand-lettering; the excess meaning in *Dr. Strangelove* is contained by neither text, nor sound, nor image. It appears through the comical implications of the design, in the use of hand-drawn "type" with odd sizes and arrangement that suggests commentary on the events shown in the live action—without *directly* making any critical or comic statement. Displacement and transformation are the hallmarks of rhetoric, making its meanings apparently natural and immediate, hiding the process that creates their significance; however, this rhetorical meaning only arises from the synthesis of text-as-language and text-as-graphics. The shifts between text-as-language and text-as-graphic are insufficient to create the allegorical meaning without their juxtaposition/superimposition over the B-52 bomber refueling. The combination of live action photography comes into this dynamic as a corollary to the shifting functions of reading::seeing, as a movement *between* understanding letters-as-text and letters-as-graphics. This instability is central to the satiric aspects of Ferro's design that foreshadow the nature and organization of the drama to follow. The rejection of text-as-meaning returns lettering to its foundation in *graphics*—shapes composed and superimposed over other, photographic materials. It is not a rejection of the ordering imposed by sight, instead being a reflexive (and thus potentially critical) reassertion of sight as organizing process that renders reading/meaning possible.

The second, complex variant of the rebus depends on precisely these instabilities between text and graphics poised in counterpoint to live action imagery: a similar dynamic of typography and montage structures Kyle Cooper's design for *Seven* (1995) produced at RGA/LA [Figure 4.9]. The shifts between graphics and text in this sequence mimic specifically mechanical camera errors: streaks and smears of the hand-scratched type reproduce the material effect of misregistrations of film in the camera as it is being shot, creating irregular flutters, streaks, and jitter on-screen. These apparent "glitches" in the exposure of the film transform the text into illegible graphics, drawing attention to it as the product of a mechanical, autonomous process subject to jams and other momentary failures. There are multiple variants of each title card, commonly juxtaposed—scratched titles on black—with close-up and extreme close-up live action photography with a minimum of overlapping superimposition between text and image. This distinction allows the live action and the typography to each receive full attention, the distinctions between title card and image remaining almost inviolate during the title sequence's 2-minute running time.

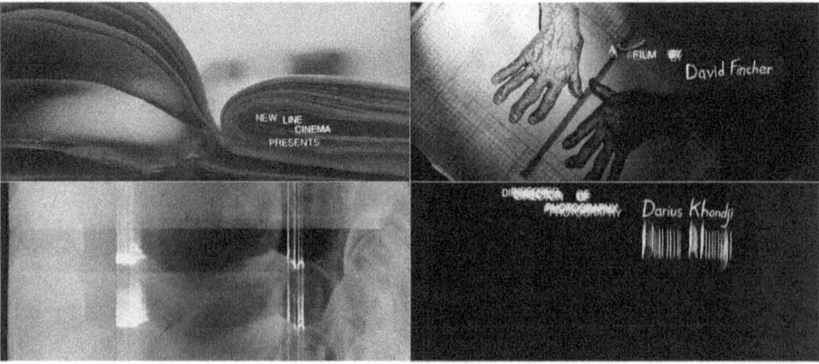

Figure 4.9 A selection of rebus title cards from *Seven* (1995)

While the clear distinction between text/image in *Seven* might appear to be a distinct approach to title sequences, the occasional superimposition and slight overlaps between title cards and live action suggest that their apparent separation may be a compromise that allows for a greater degree of graphic manipulation of the text than a more standard and consistent superimposition would allow. In spite of the distortions and "noise" introduced by the simulated mechanical errors, these title cards remain highly legible, a fact that invites a consideration of *how* the scratched-in letters shift between being graphic and language as the sequence develops. There is a tension to this design between control and catastrophe—the same ambiguity Foucault identified as the fundamental condition of the rebus: ciphers whose meaning depends on their abstraction as general signs. The difference between the credits-as-language (text) and credits-as-broken technology (streaking, jittery graphics) is a conflict between two incompatible systems of interpretation apprehending these images as signifiers of either textual information or technological failure—a pairing that uneasily coexists throughout the title sequence. The resulting tension and conflict within the title cards themselves is accentuated by both the choice of music, Nine Inch Nails's *Closer*, and the disturbing and apparently obsessive and psychotic activities shown by its synchronized live action montage.

The dominating and controlling dimensions of vision described by Foucault are readily in evidence in the background montage sequence: of particular note is the photocopied picture of a child whose eyes are blacked out with a marker; later in the sequence his entire face will be obliterated. The (extreme) close-ups function throughout this design as a focusing of attention on particular actions that, due to their isolation in each shot, assume an iconic character. Each image is fragmentary, yet when considered as a sequence, suggests repeated, obsessive activities performed over time. The insertion of title cards in between these live action shots thus act as narrative ellipses within this sequence; yet this elliptical understanding is precisely a function of their juxtaposition, the mismatch between title card and photograph—both shift ambiguously between being images and being signs for obsession and madness. This instability of the typography as text undermines the distinctions between reading and seeing that are the foundation of written language; it undermines the order this separation creates to assert a priority for the visual.

Collapsing the differences between text::image reintroduces the affect of visual design into the meaningful interpretation of titles; this concern for issues of composition, style, and dress of type is not problematic for the audience. Viewers recognize and shift between first-level and second-level interpretations fluently; these transformations are what makes these title designs noteworthy and of interest, both critically and aesthetically as audience. The shifts between an illustrative showing and a rhetorical play of signification render designs such as *Dr. Strangelove, To Kill a Mockingbird*, or *Seven* exemplary designs, recognized as noteworthy, which is the source of their influence. This mobilization of their composite structure as a reflexive commentary on the drama that follows is the idealized function for a title sequence generally.

The orchestrated modal shifts between different title cards within a singular sequence provokes a variety of distinct engagements. Unlike the figure–ground mode as in *Rumba*, the more complex engagements of text::image necessitate shifting between reading::seeing and are closely linked to the identification of a sequence as noteworthy. It is the complexity of semiosis that announces the title design as an independent production paralleling the narrative itself—this formal distinction between opening design and dramatic action reinforces the enclosed nature of the filmic "world" as separate from mundane reality. The articulation of the title sequence—even in its most basic forms—provides a demarcation which serves to identify the production as a singular unit. This isolation and relationship between title sequence and narrative is especially apparent in the conceptual-dramatic restatement of the drama within the rebus.

Notes

1 Barthes, R. "Myth Today" in *Mythologies* (New York: Noonday Press, 1970), pp. 114–116.
2 Barthes, R. "Myth Today" in *Mythologies* (New York: Noonday Press, 1970), pp. 37–39.
3 Stanitzek, G. "Reading the Title Sequence (*Vorspann, Génèrique*)." *Cinema Journal*, Vol. 48, no. 4, 2009, p. 56.
4 Stöckl, H. "Typography: Body and Dress of a Text." *Visual Communication*, Vol. 4, no. 2, June 2005, p. 78.
5 Eco, U. *The Limits of Interpretation* (Bloomington: University of Indiana Press, 1994), p. 87.
6 Eco, U. *The Limits of Interpretation* (Bloomington: University of Indiana Press, 1994), p. 98.
7 Vlaanderen, R., ed. "Iginio Lardani" in *Forget the Film, Watch the Titles*, http://www.watchthetitles.com/designers/Iginio_Lardani accessed April 16, 2013.
8 Foucault, M. *This Is Not a Pipe* (Berkeley: University of California Press, 1982), p. 44.
9 Foucault, M. *This Is Not a Pipe* (Berkeley: University of California Press, 1982), p. 21.
10 Shaheen, J. "The Detective Film in Transition." *Journal of the University Film Association*, Vol. 27, no. 2, 1975, pp. 38–39.
11 Auden, W.H. "The Guilty Vicarage" in *The Dyer's Hand and Other Essays* (New York: Vintage, 1968), p. 158.
12 Horak, J. *Saul Bass: Anatomy of Film Design* (Lexington: University of Kentucky Press, 2014), pp. 89–92.
13 McMurtrie, D. "The Philosophy of Modernism in Typography" in *Texts on Type*, ed. Steven Heller and Phillip Meggs (New York: Allworth Press, 2001), p. 147.

5

Subtitles are commonly employed to present a translation of 'foreign' languages in a motion picture. These composited texts have formal similarities to the calligram: typically placed at the bottom-center of the screen, the subtitle is accepted as having an immediate relationship to another text, either heard or seen on-screen. It is a doubling of those articulations already (natively) present in the work: understood as an *additional* text in its standard presentation on-screen, the subtitle is neither considered an integral part of the production, nor as an element of it, but is added *after*, in some cases by distribution companies that release a film in a different language—for example, a Swedish film such as *I am curious: Yellow* (1967) was released with subtitles for exhibition in the United States. In being added to the existing work, the subtitles transform the earlier composites of text and image into a single unit over and against which the subtitle appears as *another* composite: added to augment the legibility of an existing work by making its speech/writing accessible in a second language not part of that initial production.

The links between subtitles and other text/speech are paradoxically explicit and tenuous: the subtitle is recognized as being a restatement (translation), but is not a supplemental text in the conventional sense because its role is reiteration rather than additive. What the subtitle provides is not a different statement, but another "identical" statement. The implication of the subtitle's action is parenthetical, an aside addressed to only some audience members. The limited address—only some, but not all—differentiates the subtitle in a basic way from the calligram: its relationship is not to an image, but to some other text (speech/written) for which it is a doppelganger. This tautology between these different languages forms the structural relations that define the subtitle as coincident with its subject, but transformed by the change in language.

The arbitrary relation of sign and signified enables the transposition of one sign for another, provided their related meaning remains (essentially) constant. This movement between codified systems offers the fantasy of their equivalence. Being arbitrary, the transition from one system to another acts as a denial of the heterogeneous nature of language to suggest their convergence through the capacity to translate between them, a belief that reveals their assumed similarity. This action is a denial of differences; as Michel Foucault has noted, alternative systems are a threat to any established order:

> *Heterotopias* are disturbing probably because they secretly undermine language, because they make it impossible to name this *and* that, because they shatter or tangle common names, because they destroy syntax in advance, and not only the syntax with which we construct sentences but also the less apparent syntax which causes words and things (next to but also opposite one another) to "hang together."[1]

The imposed nature of the subtitle acts as a containment of the hazard that *foreign* systems always pose: the potential for a radically different ordering and meaning that contradicts familiar and established understandings. The translation from one language system into another can only be accomplished if these systems have correspondences, even if those connections are not immediately apparent "on the surface." Subtitles thus assume a reassuring form that re-aligns the disparate structures and meanings of different languages as being fundamentally identical, a denial of their alterity.

The denial of difference is always political in nature: in the case of Cary Fukunaga's design of a Levi's jeans commercial for the advertising company Wieden+Kennedy (Portland) in 2009 called *America*, the 'foreign' language is English, the same language being spoken [Figure 5.1], a doubling that reinforces the poem's suggestion that American democracy does not *necessarily* mean a uniform sameness. This short TV ad runs 60 seconds and includes eighteen text–image composites. It is part of the 2009 "Go Forth" campaign for both Levi's brand and Levi's 501 jeans. The voice reading the poem "America" from *Leaves of Grass* is rumored[2] to be Walt Whitman himself, but it leaves off the final couplet: "A grand, sane, towering, seated Mother, / Chair'd in the adamant of Time." Its source is a historical wax cylinder recording that hisses and trembles; the uncertainties of enunciation and early sound reproduction are also reproduced in the design of the subtitles themselves—scratchy, hand-drawn letters sprawl across the screen in irregular lines:

> Centre of equal daughters, equal sons,
> All, all alike endear'd, grown, ungrown, young or old,
> Strong, ample, fair, enduring, capable, rich,
> Perennial with the Earth, with Freedom, Law and Love,

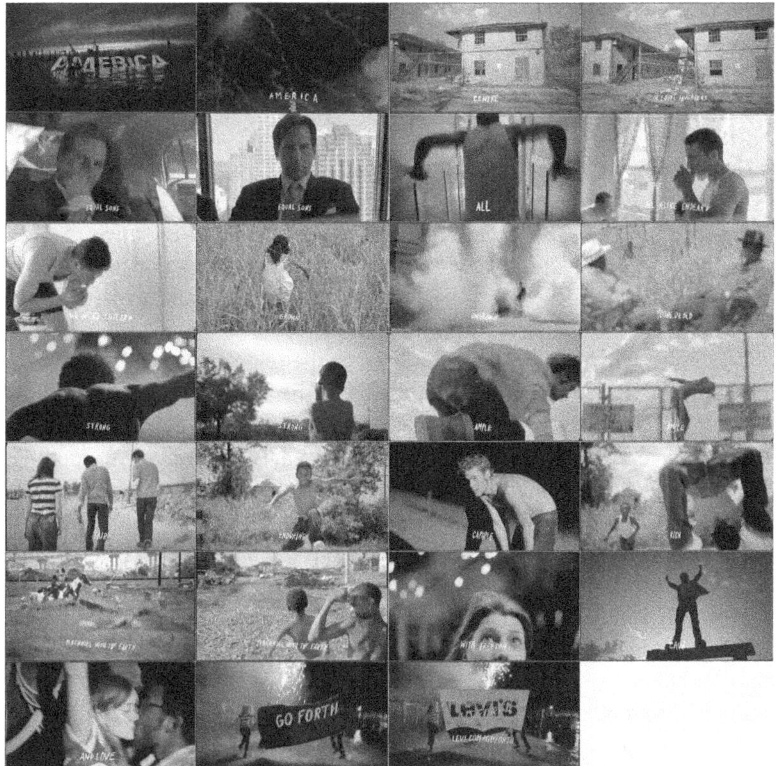

Figure 5.1 All the subtitles from *America (Go Forth)* television commercial designed by Cary Fukunaga for Wieden+Kennedy (2009)

These lines appear in fragmentary form on-screen as synchronized subtitles, appearing as the words are said, but this text is not precisely linked to the images: there are jumps where a word appears and then the images changes, or a word appears as the image cuts to an ambiguous image of smoke, fireworks, or posterized human form that it takes a second to recognize, leaving the text::image relationship uncertain. These ambivalences of this syncopation render the peculiar text::image juxtapositions coherent. Some cross multiple images, while others are connected to a single, held frame. This montage has the affect of blurring boundaries, appropriate for the poem's contents, a unification of oppositions not in dialectics but as differential points within a singular spread. These iconographic images of arcing forms have associated terms: "ALL," "STRONG," "RICH" and "LAW." The meaning these composites, and the entire commercial evoke, are populist, positive, and democratic—features also historically associated with Levi's, as anthropologist Grant McCracken notes about them both:

> If there is a brand that can claim these meanings for itself, it is Levi's. Almost everything about the brand history and heritage gives it this opportunity . . . too rarely taken up. The W+K spots do a nice job of evoking these meanings.[3]

The dislocation of subtitle and image creates composites in which the text and image often do not fully coincide, opening their connection to slippages while at the same time asserting the direct connection of hand-scratched subtitles to the accompanying voice-over. These separations act to tie the text to narration while at the same time challenging the calligram mode's assertion that the image is a visualization of the text/voice. These ruptures make the iconographic combinations' merging of *image-text-voice* more striking since they appear as singular units—examples of the rebus mode—their meaning aligned with the arcing forms: the man accompanying the subtitle "ALL" swings back and forth, bridging the narrow gap of the hall. An evocative action drawing attention to the span as a visualization of *all*, reiterating the expansive nature of the poem itself. A similar action accompanies "RICH" as the boy does a back-flip; again, an evocation of reversals and aspirations. The idea of *richness* is not necessarily connected to economics, but is instead a character trait. Finally, the "LAW" image presents a man seen from below, standing atop a crossbeam, arms upraised in a gesture commonly signifying victory, as in a boxing match. Similar actions-text–image groupings appear for "LOVE" with an interracial couple's kiss. The montage develops towards this final image that can be understood as conciliatory given the history of slavery in the United States.

The dominance of text over voice/image in this commercial renders its more peculiar images seemingly obvious and natural. The potentially divergent aspects of these materials form a singular meaning as the design consistently shifts away from calligram and figure–ground modes towards the rebus mode. As translation/transcription of the voice, the subtitles are a doubling of its statements. The style and dress of the letters as shaky, hand-drawn reiterations of the voice-over make the connection between text and voice immediately apparent, while their potential function as calligrams is mitigated by the syncopation that renders the iconographic alignments of some terms exceptions to the general organization of the commercial, masking the force of reading as an organizing activity, rendering the allusive meanings of poetry as the graphic composite of text::image. In this construction, the voice-over, central to the timing and design of the subtitles, is also secondary to them. The translation they provide gives form to the voice as not only the lexical statements, but characterized by audible features whose significance becomes more apparent when reproduced graphically in the design of the text itself. These shifts between translations of voice and calligrams reveal the hierarchies operative as pairs, text::image and text::voice, in which reading dominates its associated activity—seeing or listening. Thus, the subtitle lies at the intersection between *listening* and *seeing* mediated by *reading*. The political claims of convergence and unity reflect the *dominance* that is fundamental to the semiotics of the subtitle itself.

Subtitles and Calligrams

The subtitle is *always* imposed, not integral. This distinction in normal usage becomes apparent through its exceptions: those designs where the normal relationship of subtitle to pre-existing voice/text comes into question, in the process revealing the hierarchies and dominance the subtitle enacts. The 3.5-minute title sequence to *The Holy Grail* (1975), designed by Michael Palin, is precisely such an example of subtitles shifting the normative relationship between imposed and existing text [Figure 5.2]. This

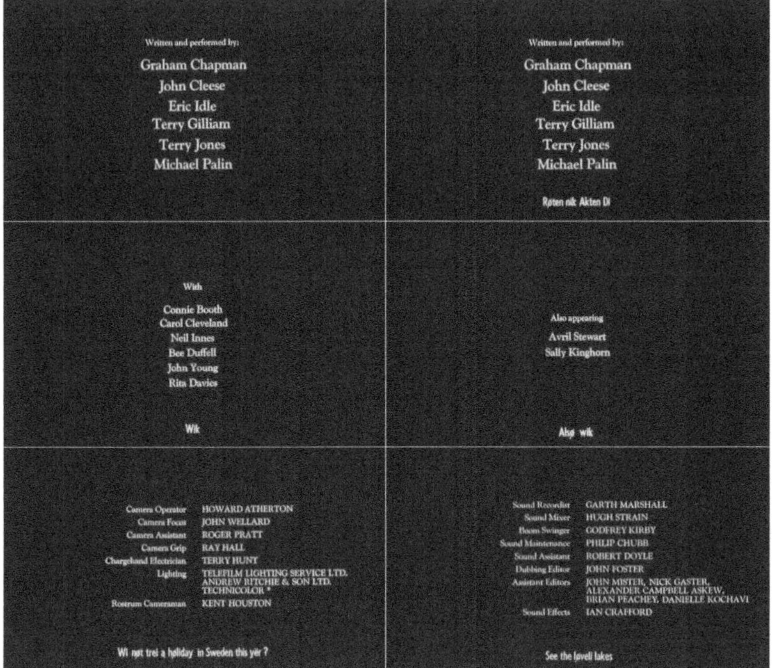

Figure 5.2 Title cards with subtitles from *The Holy Grail* (1975)

sequence is unusually long for an opening title composed exclusively from text. Its length accommodates the typical credits for production personnel expected in a film, and includes a series of subtitles that translate the English credits into "Swedish." This first 'subtitled' section lasts 2 minutes and 10 seconds of the 3.5-minute running time. The normal subtitles last only for the first two title cards (*"Wik"* and *"Alsø wik"*) before being replaced by a series of 'pseudo-subtitles' addressing the English-reading audience with pseudo-Swedish (*"Wi nøt trei a høliday in Sweden this yër?"*) that develops a comic narrative about dentistry and the dangers of moose bites in parallel to the production credits listed above.

The subtitles in *The Holy Grail* are unstable. They are organized into three sections divided by an intertitle announcing the change: the first with subtitles; the second exchanges the subtitles for disruptive insertions into the credits themselves; the third section, rendered in color, where the credits themselves have been altered. The sequence follows a clear trajectory: from a secondary text (subtitle), to additional (excess) credits in addition to the normal production credits, to finally disrupting the actual production credits. This play of text/credit, while unusual for Hollywood films and feature films generally, is not unusual for the Monty Python comedy troupe, who did similar things in the credits for their BBC TV show *Monty Python's Flying Circus* (1969–1973).[4]

The second and third sections of Palin's design, while interrupting the normal flow of credits, do not fundamentally challenge them in the way that the subtitles at the start do. These opening subtitles initially follow the standard function of subtitles: in *The Holy Grail*, they render one language, English, into another, Swedish, each shown using a different typeface. They begin slightly syncopated with the text they translate, appearing slightly after the initial English title card, a delay that encourages a recognition of these subtitles as paralleling the other text, reinforced by the different typefaces employed. Differences of language aside, they can be easily distinguished from each other visually. The words being translated—the production credits—are readily identifiable "in" the subtitle, aiding viewers in connecting the two texts, providing the essential link required for them to be "subtitles." This identification is important because, as the sequence develops, it is the idea of subtitles as "translation" that comes into question.

In shifting from being identified as-translation to "sales pitch," the subtitle reverses its subordinate position to the production credits. The distinction between subtitles and the pseudo-subtitles is immediately obvious, even though they appear in the same place on-screen. The shift is dramatic, as if the translator was "bored" with their work and decided to do something else. This changed understanding reflects the shift from passive (and foreign) status as redundant text to directly addressing the audience, in the process revealing the convergent and ultimately understood-as-coincident relationship between the translative subtitle and its subject: these texts lie within the same "field" even if they are graphically separated as distinct on-screen (i.e., they are calligrams). Unlike the typical calligram composed from text and image, the shift in language (English to Swedish) introduces a gap between one text and the other, their linkage emerging from their familiar arrangement. As in *America (Go Forth)*, the placement of subtitle at the bottom of the screen in *The Holy Grail* evokes the calligram, establishing the authority of the statements being made.

The calligram thus reveals itself as a flexible mode; not confined to relationships only with images, it always functions in the same way as a label whose power derives from repetition and redundancy. Convergent meaning establishes the calligram as reliable. Doubled meanings mutually reinforce the translation's *validity* where original text and subtitle each "prove" the other. It is a tautology. The deployment of subtitles to render speech legible is the same as using subtitles to provide translation; both are translations of a sort, each relying on the coincidence of subtitle and source. This integral relationship of subtitle to what it translates, their apparent convergence, is violated in *The Holy Grail* by shifting to direct address. The sales pitch forces the other text on-screen to be the background to its foreground—recreating the figure–ground mode's relations of dominance, but without the need for imagery. The relationships described by the figure–ground and calligram modes, while being immediately apparent when considering text::image relationships, also apply to the structural and interpretive relations of subtitles. The creation of rebus modes in subtitles, as in *America (Go Forth)*, is rare.

Diegetic and Non-Diegetic Typography

Distinguishing between text that is composed within the narrative space and text superimposed (composited) over it determines how the audience relates those words to the narrative drama. The separation of diegetic (within the story) from non-diegetic (visible to the audience, but not part of the narrative 'space') is a fundamental recognition of the conventional structure and organization of text–image composites. The shifting role for the pseudo-Swedish subtitles in *The Holy Grail* reveals this active revaluation of text–image relationships as they appear on-screen. The subtitle's shift from *imposed* to *integral* (i.e., diegetic) reflects the continuous revaluation done by audiences encountering these structures. This dynamic engagement becomes more important when considering the linkages between dramatic action and subtitles; the conventional understanding follows from the figure–ground mode's absolute separation of text and image. These independent fields come into question when the subtitles become a feature of the narrative space. The resulting design shifts, so the typography becomes a physical presence in the dramatic environment, integral—and thus no longer a parallel element, but an object within the fictive space on-screen. It is a situation that complicates Umberto Eco's comments about drama in *Interpreting Serials*:

> With words, a phonic object stands for other objects made with different stuff. In the mise-en-scene, an object, first recognized as a real object, is then assumed as a sign in order to refer to another object (or to a class of objects) whose constitutive stuff is the same as that of the representing object.[5]

The change in understanding from physical object to sign that Eco describes is a basic transformation of physical things into general signifiers—a movement away from the real presence of the thing observed, to a consideration of it as a general signifier for *all* things of a particular class (a class including the current object on view). Objects (or images of them) become connotative, rather than denotative things-themselves. This progression from physical thing to sign is a commonplace and easily recognized shift; the progression he describes is one where things become linguistic, yet there is little consideration of language (composited text) as object. The progression from language to physical object reverses this development, in the process suggesting that these texts *could be* interactive, not simply composited, but actually present in the environment.

The climactic moment of *Das Cabinet des Dr. Caligari* (*The Cabinet of Dr. Caligari*, 1919) [Figure 5.3] presents a series of such diegetic texts, each stating "DU MUSST CALIGARI WERDEN" (*"YOU MUST BECOME CALIGARI"*) that appear floating in the air and following the contours of a tree as the Director returns to his home. This sequence lasts approximately 60 seconds. It is a peculiar moment in a highly expressionist film: it is the moment the Director becomes Dr. Caligari. Even though we understand these texts are superimposed, a "camera trick," the performance suggests their *actual presence* in the on-screen dramatic space—they are an excess to that space, one the audience immediately recognizes as being a presentation of the character's internal perceptions.[6] The linguistic has become a specific, physical object within the narrative's fictional world-space. This movement is a reversal of the typical relations between specific object and general signifier—the language becomes a material thing, visible and inviting a consideration of it as something to interact with within that space. This transformation of word into object is necessary for the composited element to become a part of the 'real' space portrayed by/inside the narrative drama. The audience understands this superimposed text "DU MUSST CALIGARI

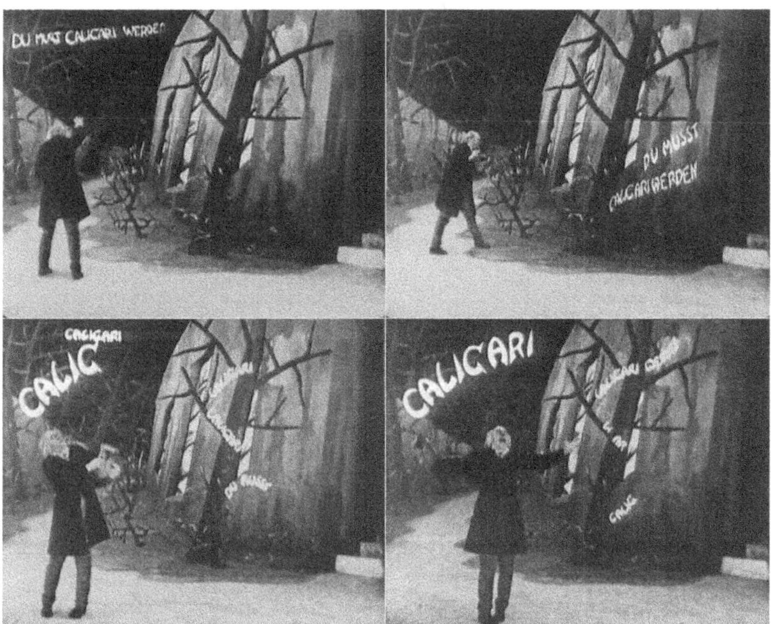

Figure 5.3 Superimposed text stating, "DU MUSST CALIGARI WERDEN" [YOU MUST BECOME CALIGARI], from *Das Cabinet des Dr. Caligari* (1919)

WERDEN" as diegetic through two contextual markers: it interacts with the on-screen environment *and* the characters within that story engage with these composited texts.

That the texts appearing in *Das Cabinet des Dr. Caligari* are "fantasy/psychosis," an expression of deranged senses signifying insanity through their narrative action returns these texts through the symbolic transformation Eco describes: they signify the Director's new-born madness; their appearance is an externalization of his mind onto the environment, an action these texts dramatize. In watching this sequence, these texts are clearly present in the space and "not really" there. Their appearance gives the audience a privileged view into the character's perceptions—a recognition that can only happen once these words-become-objects return to the symbolic realm, not as the verbal statement they contain, but as a cipher for madness. Words no longer represent (connote) what they state when they become *objects* contained and interactively engaged in a fictional environment; in becoming objects, they enable a new understanding independent of their lexical meaning. This potential for transformed meaning, a secondary articulation separate from their lexical meaning, develops from these words' denial of the figure–ground mode's separation of text and image into overlapping, but mutually exclusive, fields. By crossing this boundary, the lexical functions of language detach from the text—its lexical content is simply a denotation of what these particular words happen to state in this part of the screen-world—a necessary rupture that defies the organization of the motion picture as so much image accompanied by so much text. The parallel realms coincide, asserting that these words appearing on-screen are integral, not superimposed. In the process of becoming diegetic, this fusion denies the interpretive modes that normatively distinguish text from image. While they are technically superimposed, their narrative role *within* the diegesis prevents their consideration via figure–ground or calligram modes: the objectified text is no longer engaged as text, but as physicality, present for the characters and thus open to symbolic interpretation separate from its meaning as text.

Diegetic Subtitles

The last of the "Austin Powers" films produced in the 1990s and 2000s, *Goldmember* (2002) contains a short sequence that 'plays' with the standard conventions of subtitles: the 'foreign language' being subtitled is Japanese [Figure 5.4]. This imposed translation into English shifts to become

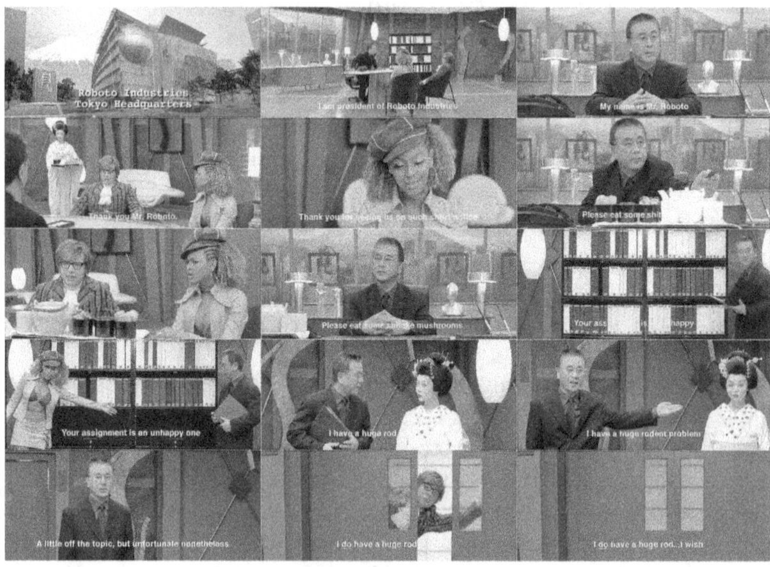

Figure 5.4 Subtitles from the "Mr. Roboto" sequence in *Goldmember* (2002)

the focus of the scene's narrative content—these subtitles are not invisible to the characters appearing on-screen. The translated dialogue produces a self-referential moment where apparently scatological statements reveal the differential between what is said and what is written—this mise-en-scene the source of its comic effect. However, this recognition sets in motion a series of modal shifts where the meaning of these subtitled translations come into doubt in a direct fashion: the "hidden" naughtiness of banal statements which are animated by the live action characters' interaction with the superimposed typography draws attention to the series of 'mis'statements, each revealed as an illusion created by the composition of white subtitle text in relation to the white objects in the background image: the narrative mise-en-scene embeds the subtitles diegetically while they are clearly superimposed.

The re-interpretation of non-sequitur as scatology draws attention to the potential mismatches between translation and statement—the characters' commentary and interaction with the subtitles focuses directly on this mistranslation in an explicit fashion—invoking the same problematics that Foucault identifies in the apparent conflict created by Rene Magritte's painting *The Treachery of Images*, in which a realistic painting of a pipe is subtitled with a statement that "this is not a pipe" effectively drawing attention to the normative functions of calligramic language through its denial, shifting from a first-level statement to the second relational meaning. This same dynamic comes into play with these subtitles. Because they rapidly shift between being non-diegetic and diegetic, the interaction becomes the subject of the sequence, as in Palin's design for *The Holy Grail*.

The presence of these texts is established by Power's comment that he doesn't speak Japanese but reads the subtitles, initiating the series of self-referential jokes.

Earlier in *Goldmember*, another sequence also addresses the issues of subtitles-as-translation [Figure 5.5]. In this sequence where Powers and his Father ("Nigel Powers" played by Michael Caine) speak "English English"—a dialogue initially composed from British slang that rapidly decays into both verbal and written incoherence. In this case, the subtitles are *not* diegetic—the women seated on the bed cannot understand what the Powers are saying; neither can the translator. The breakdown in subtitles begins as a peculiar non-sequitur, the statement that reads, "A lawyer who became a policeman in a truck . . . " is followed by a block reading "??????????"; the subtitles never return to coherence, even when the translation does resume. Uncertainty about the words said renders their translation impossible, just as problems with the superimposition of the type creates scatological nonsense statements whose meaning is radically different. In both cases, the hierarchy of text as dominant in these calligrams comes into question.

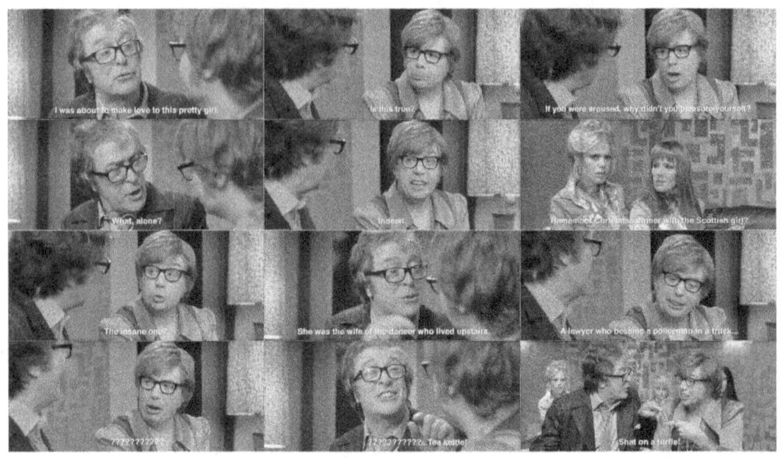

Figure 5.5 Subtitles from the "English English" sequence in *Goldmember* (2002)

The regimented meaning that a subtitle provides—an assertion of certainty—is what both "Mr. Roboto" and "English English" demonstrate in different ways. The legibility of the text itself in the "Mr. Roboto" sequence challenges the relation of subtitle to normative language, leaving the functioning of the calligram intact, but only if the changed meaning can be accepted as provisionally accurate. The "English English" sequence also suggests the same immediate transfer as in "Mr. Roboto," created instantaneously as the dramatic scene proceeds. Yet in providing a dysfunctional translation, the "English English" sequence collapses into incoherence during some joke shared between these characters; the "joke" is on the audience. These subtitles do not provide a privileged view and understanding of what is happening on-screen, forcing the audience into an awareness of its artificiality. The calligram's transparent link becomes an obstacle to understanding the scene. This shift makes the conventional nature of the calligram's organization of meaning into a self-consciously imposed statement. For the subtitles that *fail* to translate this scene, what appears is not a calligram, but a rebus—although it is one whose resolution requires recognition of the arbitrary nature of the translation. Once this recognition happens, there can be no comfortable return to the calligram, and the sequence comes to an end as the dialectic has presented itself as such.

Comedy films are particularly useful in considering challenges to established conventions in cinema. Divergence from established hierarchies commonly appears in comedy because there is an expectation for challenges to established authority, even if that challenge is automatically dismissed by the designation "comedy." What appears in question in satire and parody is secretly affirmed by the clear absurdity, inappropriateness, and ridiculous character presented through comedy—it is not a challenge, but an assertion that the established order is the only coherent one, the natural organization of the world. The hierarchy thus perpetuated finds itself affirmed through the superficial opposition of the jokes made. The apparent paradox of the anticipated (even expected) violation of propriety is resolved by the assimilation of these violations to the order they superficially subvert. That assertion through denial renders these challenges to the established function of subtitles theoretically useful: they reveal their conventional nature, but do not replace it. What appears subversive is an establishment of these structures with greater certainty because they do not offer an alternative—in demonstrating *how* the order breaks down, that order becomes all the more secure. Michel Foucault's observations about the *pipe* in Magritte's paintings reveals this process as an active re/assertion of meaning rendered visible on-screen.

Subtitles use the calligram mode because, as in the title sequence, subtitled text is dependent on an intertextual relationship to the narrative for its significance, yet unlike the paratext, the subtitle is essential to its interpretation, rendering access to content that might not otherwise be comprehensible. In attacking this function, the two scenes in *Goldmember* reveal the artifice that lies in the background to the production as a whole—but both sequences demonstrate the fabricated nature of the "reality on film" in such a way that they do not undermine it, instead asserting its autonomy from the realist presentation shown on-screen. The inability to translate, just as much as the problems with mise-en-scene, only become coherent as events if we accept the 'space' on-screen and its fictional world as internally consistent and separate from the particular views afforded by the film. This assimilation, even dependence, of both scenes on their realism's veracity prevents the challenges posed by the violation of established conventions from turning into an essential challenge to the narrative drama itself. This reversion to the realist order returns the subtitles to the drama that is central to the events, enabling both sequences' revelations that *create* the comedy.

Notes

1 Foucault, M. *This Is Not a Pipe* (Berkeley: University of California Press, 1982), p. 4.

2 Hummer, T.R. "Edison and Poetry: Did Edison Record Walt Whitman?" *The Edisonian*, Vol. 10, February 2013, http://edison.rutgers.edu/newsletter10.html#5 accessed July 4, 2016.

3 McCracken, G. "Walt Whitman and the Levi's Ad." October 29, 2009, http://cultureby.com/2009/10/walt whitman.html accessed July 4, 2016.
4 Johnson, K. *The First 20 Years of Monty Python* (New York: Diane Publishing Company, 1989).
5 Eco, U. *The Limits of Interpretation* (Bloomington: Indiana University Press, 1994), p. 104.
6 Betancourt, M. *The History of Motion Graphics: From Avant-Garde to Industry in the United States* (Rockport: Wildside Press, 2013).

6

The Importance of Theory

Theorizing the semiotics of text and image when they are composited together on-screen is not only or exclusively a concern for title sequences, but is a recurring issue for motion graphics as a whole. That the peculiar dynamics of how past experiences and immanent encounter interact to create meaning is fundamentally unconsidered and untheorized is part of a general refusal of theorization by the design fields. However, the need for a consideration of these structures increases with each new technology that makes the combination of text and image on-screen a commonplace part of the contemporary world. Title sequences were the focus of the present study because they are the most immediately recognized and generally considered site for these composites, yet the conventional wisdom about their history, structure, and meaning has been primarily concerned with how the title sequence can be related to the dramatic narrative that follows. The semiotics of these text–image composites have been neglected and ignored in favor of the understanding of titles exclusively as paratexts, an understanding initially proposed by designers such as Saul Bass, Maurice Binder, Dan Perri, or Kyle Cooper as an explanation and justification for their own work. The critical tendency when considering title sequences has been to focus on exactly these *artistic* works, leading to the false belief that film title design was not a significant concern prior to the "revolutionary" work of Saul Bass in the mid-1950s, and that only those designs with an auteur have merit. Complex and dynamic forms appear in title sequences throughout the history of motion pictures in the United States, yet these designs tend towards anonymity rather than being the featured work of credited/recognized artist-designers such as Bass. In selecting examples for this discussion, what was prioritized was not the designer who made the sequence, but its ability to serve as an example of each *mode*: the design's capacity to demonstrate a general principle or typical approach. This decision was self-conscious. The focus in this discussion was on the articulation of meaning and how these meanings depend *not* on prescriptive lexia, but the ambivalences of audience identifications, past experience/expertise, and the cultural dominance of written language over visual encounter.

Title sequences have been and always will be a subservient, liminal form—literally at the margin between where the narrative begins and the production logos, film trailers, commercials, and other materials shown as part of the same program. Much has been made of them as *paratexts* because of this liminal boundary—how to start the film, with credits or without, using an elaborate independent sequence, integrating the title design with the often essential film preamble, or choosing instead a simple title-card-only opening that allows for a rapid entry into the narrative drama. These different aesthetics employ the same small set of underlying assumptions about the emergence of meaning from the (unexamined) dynamics of text and image, demonstrating the need for a theory of how these modes' organizational functions produce semiosis.

Formal relationships described by each mode inflect the meaning immediately, opening or closing the audience's conception of how the text relates to the imagery. The composite nature of these modes lends them a broader scope than merely a description of text::image relationships in the title sequences for motion pictures: they can be recognized even in still form (as the various film stills in this book testify). Through these composited elements, the distinct fields of motion graphics and graphic design converge on a shared set of semiotic protocols for interpretation. What is important to recognize about the figure–ground, calligram, and rebus modes is they do not depend on photography for their production of meaning; it is sufficient that the elements combined belong to different fields—text and image, or even distinctions between one language and another—to be held apart in the mind so the relational linkages specific to the semiotic forms described in this study can emerge. Their shifting meanings rely on the particulars of encounter: audience recognitions of text::image relationship follows conventional associations learned in childhood through picture books and word play.

Text::image composites follow from precisely these established arrangements present as a deflection of meaning by countering one term with another, through quotation and allusion to other, implicitly remembered texts and internalized, formal associations. Thus the play of the text::image is part of the same rhetorical range in any encounter with meaning: it depends on these grammatical and lexical associations, all of which are degrees of intertextual cultural knowledge, to organize the materials into the hierarchy that it is theory's task to identify and explain. In producing a fundamental account of their dynamics and organization, it becomes possible to understand *why* they appear as they do.

The Irrelevance of Productive Technologies

The semiotic modes that render meaning in the title sequence are constrained historically by the technology used in their production only in terms of how often the rebus mode appears in title designs. The emergence of digital tools enables these modes to become an increasingly common part of media, making the need for a theoretical analysis increasingly obvious. However, in spite of the digital revolution making kinetic typography inexpensive and easily made, it still depends on a specific, limited set of tools that enable its production. The initial development of optical printing in 1929 offered a similar "revolution" in quality and variety, allowing the production of radically new kinds of visual imagery in motion, but the semiotics of text::image do not change precisely because of this heritage imposed by the technical limits of this technology. Distinctions in production technology from 1929, when optical printing was introduced, until the mid-1990s, when digital systems began replacing it—first the animation stand and optical printer, then the character generator and television studio—all the historical technologies have been replaced by the digital computer, which brings greater precision, a broader range of technical processes, and reduced cost to the production of kinetic typography and motion design generally. The selection of designs considered in this study demonstrate that these technologies are merely a means, since the semiotics of these text::image composites remain constant despite the technological changes.

Neither do the innovations of design produced by Saul Bass in the 1950s change these underlying techniques: his work is as a stylist, adapting Modernist design for motion picture title sequences, not as an inventor of new structural models. *Carmen Jones* (1954) employs superimposed text over a long take of flames composited with a graphic of a rose; *The Man with the Golden Arm* (1955) is a limited cel animation of static lines—the only animated parts are transitions—that morph into the famous, iconic arm at the very end for the "directed by Otto Preminger" title card. Aside from the graphic design employed in the arrangement of type and animated elements, these titles are not technically different from works produced in 1930 or 1920: the Modernist graphic style is what distinguishes Bass's titles from earlier designs. This distinction between design and technical production is significant since it enables a separation of productive means from the expressive contents of those works, while at the same time making the semiotics of these designs an entirely different issue, unrelated to either aesthetics or technology.

The mediating role of compositing—produced by optical printing or digitally—makes an understanding of the photographic techniques and methods of optical printing that were essential to the design and technical creation of most title sequences prior to the introduction of digital systems no longer an important consideration. Visualizing and designing complex arrangements of animation and live action with optical printers was often a fraught process, limiting the possibilities for the development of the more complex varieties of the rebus mode, a limitation on the range of semiotic modes by the technology itself that becomes more apparent when looking at older productions. The title designer Maurice Binder explained the difficulties of working with physical film to create the complex designs seen in his work on the James Bond film series:

> There's about eight layers of film to make one frame, practically. That's why if there's changes made or the music is different or something like that, it means cutting into eight pieces of film and changing it all again, which is very difficult. So you shoot in color for the backgrounds and you shoot in silhouette for the girls. Then there's the superimposition for the other effects. And then on top of that you put the titles. That's another thing superimposed on top. If you shoot everything in color you can only go a certain range. Where in *Thunderball* I shot everything in black and white—the girls were silhouettes against white and the water was silhouette against black. Then I combined the color in the optical print and then you filter and do anything you want.[1]

The limited number of discrete, physical elements used to make even one frame of Binder's titles for the *Bond* openings reflects the limitations imposed by working with composite photography in an optical printer. His working method necessarily seems clumsy compared to the immediacy of digital systems where it is simple to create highly detailed and seamless pre-visualizations of planned composites. There is no need to struggle with the limits of a physical medium as Binder does. Digital systems enable a fluid and continuous manipulation. Nevertheless, the aesthetics and technical constraints on text–image composites that emerge from optical printing are still in evidence in contemporary digital title designs. What has changed is the technology of their production, not the semiotics of text::image relations on-screen. This constancy of semiotic modes is reiterated by their ease-of-comprehension by audiences. The directness and simplicity of apparent connection-relations these modes describe challenges their identification and analysis precisely because their normative function masks the ideological roles of established knowledge and expertise that renders the modes "transparent."

The Constraints of Narrative Function

Critically addressing title sequences is complicated by narrative conventions. Integration into the film narrative is a potential with any of the three semiotic modes, depending only on the audience recognizing that the film's narrative has begun. Both *Rumba* (1936) and *Touch of Evil* (1958) employ the figure–ground mode composited with a long take as the background image, yet there is no confusion about the relationship between events shown during the titles and those of the drama in *either* film opening. A paratext always finds itself rendered subordinate to the central text, however complex and dramatic it might be on its own: the distinction between a direct and an indirect connection to the dramatic narrative reveals the underlying conception of the motion image itself, not merely the technical capacities of its production, nor only the limitations of fictional versus documentary narratives. The shift from title sequence into film narrative is a complex transformation, one that is not equally apparent over the history of title designs. The differences between *Rumba* and *Touch of Evil* become apparent immediately on examination: in *Touch of Evil*, the figure–ground mode titles appear superimposed over the *unoccupied* space on-screen—empty space where there is no activity happening, thus establishing this background image as of equal significance to the typography. In contrast, *Rumba*'s titles are centered and frequently obliterate the live action background—they obstruct and prevent any clear identification of the actions shown in the background during this long take; in *Touch of Evil*, these background actions are always readily apparent. Other distinctions also emerge in *Touch of Evil*: there is a dramatic element to these titles—their 3-minute run-time from the start to the explosion is a real-time presentation that makes the audience *wait* for the bomb in the car trunk to explode—this singular take is significantly longer than the duration required for just the title cards; the space it traverses is populated by a variety of actors performing a pageant of street activities as the shot follows this waiting-to-explode car, never fully losing track of it. The narrative meanings commonly provided by montage appear instead through the real-time continuous action (long take) that evokes documentary form.

The narrative function for title sequences depends on the same proximate decisions about relations that distinguish the calligram from the figure–ground mode: an identification of meaning *in* the image-sequence that is independent of their role and activity *as* background for the type. These mechanics of composition and compositing are autonomously recognized and understood; they do not require a conscious decision to decode or identify this hierarchy, making their disentanglement an operation of distinguishing between subtleties that seem insignificant in themselves. This recognition is qualitatively different from the meanings that might emerge from this opening *as* title sequence: the definition of "bad girl" in *Bad Girls Go to Hell* (1965) provided by the opening montage does not enable or encourage a confusion of the title sequence with the narrative in the way that *Touch of Evil* necessarily does.

Drama offers an insistent rejoinder to the obviously designed aspects of the title sequence: once the opening of the narrative and the title sequence merge, the historical aesthetic claim that the title sequence functions as a mediating transition between "real life" and the stylized realism of film collapses. The illusion of the film world being a continuous, independent reality that is revealed by camera and motion picture may lead to an aesthetic constructed from continuous camera runs (long takes), yet these rarely find any application in Hollywood film outside the title sequence—as a background for superimposed text. The duration of long takes in title sequences is typically the same (or nearly so) as the duration needed for the type placement within that long take: the duration of the long take and its use in the title historically are the same.

The distinction between titles/narrative depends as much on the dominant ideology as on particular aesthetic conceptions of motion pictures—whether realism, animation, or illustration—that authorizes the particular choices made: the nature of the design in *Touch of Evil* asserts a significance for the photography as being equal to the text, yet remains within the figure–ground mode's orchestration of text and image as independent fields of comprehension. Their equality allows the dramatic elements to emerge, directing the audience's attention to the contents of the long take as more significant than mere background. The importance of narrative function for the title sequence is not only a matter of text::image relations, but establishes the role of the title sequence in relation to the rest of the film. The paratextual approach to title sequences renders the idea of an "independent title sequence" illogical, since the titles can be related to the narrative in some fashion, however oblique that link might be. But subordinate paratexts that integrate the title into the opening of the film's drama, beyond the contractual need for crediting the actors and other production personnel, resolves perceived conflicts with the desire to immediately begin the film that the "independent title sequence" sometimes has.

However, narrative relations are tangential to the semiotics of text::image structures, and the rebus mode produces meaning in excess to the title's narrative function; identifying additional meanings for these integrated openings, as in *Bullitt*, requires a second level of signification, the rebus, to transform the narrative elements into something more complex. This excess emerges from the implicit hierarchy of reading::seeing expressed by shot duration, composition, and title card design. In transitioning to this second level of signification, the distinction between an opening title that is narrative and one that is a designed sequence requires the audience to choose to consider the opening as potentially presenting an excess of meaning; while such a consideration is always a potential, those designs that employ the rebus mode, as in *Bullitt*, invite these additional considerations by identifying their designed-status while at the same time presenting their dramatic contents as the primary focus.

In telling stories, the narrative demands ultimately dominate, even if at individual moments during this opening the text takes a central position—the priority of reading over seeing may be fleeting, but in the moments of its dominance, it is total. This dynamic brings the hierarchy described by Foucault into practice. Each title card's text dominates the image it accompanies, but when orchestrated within a dramatic opening, the narrative function is more powerful, subordinating all the title cards to its unifying action. What one remembers about the opening of *Bullitt* is less about the masking than about the montage it presents—the start of the drama itself.

The subordinate nature of a title design is also its guarantee of innate complexity. The assessment and interpretation of title designs is never only as an independent entity, but in context with the material that follows and all the cultural associations that precede it, leaving the interpretation of title sequences as the product of these intersections of past knowledge and anticipation of what is to come. This liminal nature helps explain the historical lack of consideration given to the title sequence. Interpretation of these designs can be perplexing precisely because they are unstable, each design seemingly an answer to unique demands, leading to a focus on the solutions produced by "star" designers. What provides the interpretive and aesthetic interest of these designs emerges from how the designer has adapted conventional resolutions to appear singular and independent. Yet this approach addresses only part of how audiences engage the design, neglecting exactly those established solutions that make the credited designer's work innovative. By addressing more basic structures of meaning and organization in the design—the reading::seeing dynamic and the various modes that emerge from it—the complexity of title sequences becomes quantifiable as shifting relationships between showing and telling that depend on the audience's established expertise, transferred from earlier encounters in childhood with text–image combinations. Interpreting a title sequence depends on this encultured expertise.

Both the calligram and rebus modes' transformation of the figure–ground mode rely on an immanent connection of text–image that the audience makes without thinking. These complex modes depend on their autonomous application; thus on established, cultural foundations that function semantically to prioritize and organize perception. Separate from and independent of whatever technical solutions are employed in its creation, any composited text–image structure becomes coherent only through conventionally governed lexia that are only partly based in consistent arrangements on-screen, but require an equal support via their audience's past expertise developed in childhood with the calligrams and rebuses of picture books. This hierarchy created around the dynamics of reading::seeing—words dominating image—creates the foundation for the ambiguities and rhetorical shifts that make title designs fun.

Note

1 Sulski, Jim. "Giving Credits Where Credits Are Due." *Fantastic Films*, Vol. 2, no. 7, January 1980, Issue 13, p. 36.

Index